The WOMEN'S GOLF HANDBOOK

The WOMEN'S GOLF HANDBOOK

The complete guide to improving your game

VIVIEN SAUNDERS

MARSHALL PUBLISHING • LONDON

A Marshall Edition
Conceived by
Marshall Editions Limited
The Orangery
161 New Bond Street
London W1Y 9PA

First published in the UK in 2000 by Marshall
Publishing Ltd
Copyright © 2000 Marshall Editions
Developments Ltd.

ISBN 1-84028-315-7

Originated in Singapore by Master Image
Printed in Dubai by Oriental Press

Project Editor Guy Croton
Art Editor Glen Wilkins
Picture Research Caroline Watson
Managing Editor Wendy James
Managing Art Editor Patrick Carpenter
Editorial Director Ellen Dupont
Art Director Dave Goodman
Editorial Coordinator Ros Highstead
Production Amanda Mackie

Cover credits: photography Laura Wickenden,
Allsport/Andrew Redington, Peter Dazeley;
Illustration Focus Publishing

10 9 8 7 6 5 4 3 2 1

Contents

Introduction

Vivien Saunders was the first European woman to qualify for the US Tour and British Ladies Open Champion in 1977. She owns two highly successful golf courses in England and keeps an eye on the national teams of several countries. She has twice been British Sports Coach of the Year and was awarded an OBE in 1977 for services to golf.

Whether you are a beginner or a scratch player – or even a non-golfer who is enthralled by watching the game – the *Women's Golf Handbook* has something for everyone.

Obviously the ideal way to learn or play is out on the course or on the practice ground, but no matter what your standard you will find the *Women's Golf Handbook* an invaluable guide.

This specially designed book with its lavish use of photographs and diagrams takes you through the very basics, introducing you to the sport and to its terminology and rules. For the advanced golfer there are many tips on technique and thinking to give you a greater understanding of winning and scoring.

Every page is enhanced with key thoughts to remember when you're polishing up your style or playing a tournament. Golf is a wonderful game. It can be learnt by anyone from the age of six to 80. Many women take up the sport in their 50s and 60s and are still able to reach a good standard of play. The great advantage of golf is that it has a handicap system. This allows the comparative novice to compete with players of a far higher standard. It is a game where men and women can compete on equal terms, with the assistance of their handicaps and different lengths of courses.

There are now probably more than 10 million women golfers throughout the world, with courses in almost every country offering magnificent settings and challenges. They are places where great friendships are made.

If you haven't played the game before, then I hope this book will give you a thoroughly enjoyable introduction to golf.

If you are an experienced golfer, I'm sure you will be an even better one by the time you reach the very last page!

Happy golfing!

Vivien Saunders
Abbotsley, St Neots, Cambridgeshire
www.ladiesgolf.co.uk

Women's Golf – A Short Review

No one knows the precise origins of the game of golf. Some suggest it began in medieval times, with shepherds hitting pebbles round a hillside with their crooks to while away the hours spent tending sheep.

Another suggestion is that the game derived from the ancient Flemish pastime of chole, which was already known about and played in England by the mid-14th century.

Perhaps the most likely forerunner was the Dutch game of *kolf,* documented as early as the end of the 13th century and portrayed in many Dutch landscape paintings by the 16th century. 'Golfers' certainly played across country with a stick and ball, not into a hole but to certain landmarks, usually doors on specific buildings.

It was in Scotland, however, that the game of golf really developed. Up and down the east coast it apparently became so popular a pastime that in 1457 James II, in an Act of Parliament, banned golf – and football too – because these sports were interfering with archery practice. Skill with a bow and arrow was crucial to keeping the English out of Scotland.

The game remained uniquely Scottish – perhaps along with the Dutch kolf – until James VI of Scotland also became King of England and took the game south with him. At Blackheath, in south London, the Scottish nobleman laid out a seven hole course so he and his court could continue playing their beloved game.

The early courses in Scotland bore little resemblance to those of today. The game was played over public land – as in places it still is – with natural hazards and obstacles to negotiate. Not only were walls and ditches part of the game, but players often had to thread their way through others who were out enjoying their various recreations – horse racing, cricket, picnicking and so on.

The first known woman golfing enthusiast was Catherine of Aragon, the first wife of Henry VIII. Catherine wrote about her interest in the game but sadly spent so much time being pregnant in an attempt to deliver a male heir to the British throne, that her participation in the sport was clearly limited! At the end of the 20th century there are still bastions of male golf where the attitude that a woman's place is in the home continues to this day!

Mary Queen of Scots, however, had a more enlightened attitude. She was reprimanded at her trial for treason for playing golf just two days after the death of her philandering husband, Darnley.

Quite when women's golf blossomed, we do not know. It was certainly being played by the fishermen's wives of Musselburgh on the East coast of Scotland, in the latter half of the 18th century. They were probably not as efficient administrators as are many of today's women golfers and their record keeping was non-existent. The first documented clubs were the St Andrews Ladies Golf Club, started in 1867, and the Westward Ho! Club in Devon, started in 1868.

The Ladies Golf Union was formed in 1893, by which time there were over 50 ladies' golf clubs throughout the country. Golf spread throughout America and the British Commonwealth Countries. In 1930 the first Curtis Cup Match was held – sponsored by American sisters Harriot and Margaret Curtis – for a match between the amateur women golfers of USA and Great Britain. Professional golf for women expanded throughout the US from 1950 and throughout Europe, Australia and Asia from the 1970s.

Despite the enormous popularity of the game amongst women, there are still many clubs today where women are decidedly second-class citizens. As late as 1975 the Professional Golfers Association in the UK had a rule which stated quite simply that women members should have the same rights as men, save that they could not play in tournaments, attend meetings or vote! At other clubs women are barred from playing until after, for example, 4 o'clock in the afternoon, on Saturdays. At some clubs women have the status of associates rather than full members. Others display signs such as 'no dogs or women in front of the clubhouse'. Fortunately, with legislation and a more enlightened view towards women, rules and traditions are changing – though clubs still remain in both the US and UK where a divorced woman is not accepted for membership, where women cannot hold shares or vote at the club and where single women are not admitted at all.

Laura Davies One of the longest hitters in the women's game, Laura Davies of England has been a leading player worldwide for a number of years and a great ambassador for the sport in general.

At the end of the 20th century the two leading women golfers in the world were neither British nor American. Karrie Webb of Australia was the undisputed Number 1 player and Annika Sorenstam of Sweden was her closest contender. Both are from countries where the status of women golfers is equal to that of men.

In other countries, Catherine of Aragon would find few clubs today with creche facilities to enable her to participate in the sport as a young mum. Mary Queen of Scots (despite her royal title) would find herself barred from membership of the Royal and Ancient Golf Club at St Andrews. She might even find some clubs demanding her resignation due to her status as a widow!

Getting Started

Women's strengths and weaknesses at the game of golf are very different from those of men. Most women have more mobility and learn a stylish golf swing more easily. Women's problems tend to be in contact and distance, while men, as a rule, have a better eye for a ball, getting a good contact, and are better at judging depth and distance.

If you have never played the game before, walk around with an experienced player, or pull her trolley. This will give you some idea of the basics of etiquette, teach you where to stand and introduce you to the golf clubs and some of the essential golfing terms.

Your first two or three lessons can be the most important of your career. The ideal place to start is at a driving range with a pay-and-play course or, even better, a short par 3 course. The professional staff can give you tuition on the range and guide you into starting on the golf course.

But, first things first. In this chapter you find out all you need to know about the different types of golf club and how to kit yourself out.

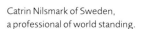

Catrin Nilsmark of Sweden,
a professional of world standing.

Choosing Your Golf Clubs

The clubs you use on the course will change depending on how quickly you advance in the game. It is better to start with a few and to learn to use each one well, rather than to have too many clubs and not be able to distinguish between them.

In the past there was no restriction on the number of clubs you could carry. Old photographs from the 1940s show caddies in America struggling to carry up to 30 different clubs! Today the golfer is limited to a maximum of 14, but there is still an element of choice. Manufacturers produce sets comprising five woods, the clubs for distance, and 11 irons, designed to produce a range of distances, from which you make your choice, together with a putter.

Women beginners should start with a few clubs – a half set. This should comprise a 3 wood, 7 wood, 5 iron, 7 iron, 9 iron, sand

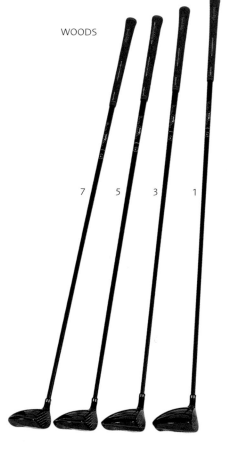

WOODS

7   5   3   1

The heads of putters come in a variety of different shapes. Which you choose is very much a matter of personal preference. Experiment before making your selection.

The degree of loft of a club face is the main factor in the distance attainable with that club. As a rule, the lower the number of the club, the lower the loft of the face – and the further it will hit the ball.

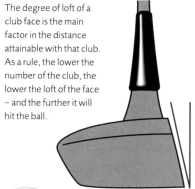

REMEMBER
START WITH
A FEW CLUBS
YOU CAN
ADD TO

wedge and putter. Ideally, ask your professional to help you choose clubs you can add to as you gain more experience. Or you can trade in that half set within two years or so, as you improve.

For the average woman golfer, the ideal full set is: a driver (1 wood) and 3, 5 and 7 woods; 3, 4, 5, 6, 7, 8 and 9 irons; a pitching wedge (P, below) and sand wedge (S, below); and a putter. Both the driver and the 3 iron can be difficult clubs for average players. Many women professionals no longer use a 3

iron, preferring instead a 7 wood which covers much the same distance. Most women find the 7 wood easier. Some manufacturers make a 2 wood, which has slightly more loft and can be an easier club to use than a driver. A good short set for a higher handicap player would be the 3, 5 and 7 woods, together with the irons from 4 iron to sand wedge – and, of course, the putter.

Putters come in all shapes and sizes, materials and colours. Choose one particularly suited for women.

Some golfers favour the 'broom-handle' putter pictured here. In theory the longer handle and accentuated pendulum-swing of the club can help overcome putting problems.

IRONS

3   4   5   6   7   8   9   P   S

The Design of Clubs

Knowing why and how clubs differ from one another will help
you select the ones that are best for you. Always select those
made specifically for women – unless you are particularly
strong, a player of championship standard or very tall. Men's
clubs are usually far too heavy for the average woman player.

In many ways the shaft of the club is the
most important part. The materials being
used in club manufacture are constantly
changing. Look for a light shaft – titanium
or graphite. If the shaft is too stiff the
tendency is for poor height and shots
finishing to the right. This is the main
danger if you use men's clubs. If the shaft is
too weak and flexible, it may lead to erratic
direction. Don't use stiff shafts unless you
are sure you can cope with them.

Irons – the head shapes
The type of irons you use can dictate the
height you get with shots. They can also
control direction. A club weighted at the
bottom of the clubhead will tend to hit the
ball higher. One with weight at the back
would tend to hit the ball lower.
    The design of the head can also affect the
direction of shots. An offset club is designed
to cure a slice. The head is set well back from
the shaft. The tendency with this is to line up
the end of the toe and the neck of the club.
The club then tends to close and eliminates
shots slicing to the right.
    Large-headed irons are easier to use. Most
golf clubs now have weight distributed at the
toe and heel. Heel and toe weighting extends
the sweet spot and gives greater tolerance for
a mis-hit shot.

Offset woods
It is possible to buy offset woods as well as
offset irons. An offset wood has the same
effect as an offset iron, in that it helps to
eliminate slicing to the right.

The angle of loft increases through the set
of woods and irons to allow progressively
higher and shorter shots. There is a 1.25cm
(½in) difference between adjacent clubs.
This change in length is combined with the
grading to the lie. The pitching wedge sits the
most upright of the irons, with the long irons
and the woods the flattest. The lie sometimes
has to be varied for taller or shorter players.

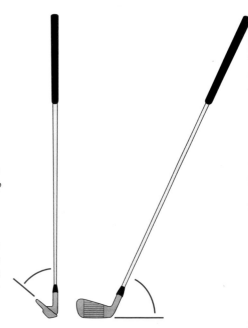

The angle of loft (left) increases with the number of
the club and affects the length of the shot. Similarly,
the angle of grading to the lie of the club head (right)
varies from club to club and also affects the length
that shots may be hit with a particular club.

WHAT THE TERMS MEAN

Shaft

Socket

Toe

Heel

Back

Head

Shaft

Socket

Face

Shaft

Loft

Grooves

Socket

Hosel

Toe

Sole

Offset head

Shaft

Socket

Hosel

Heel

Leading edge

The illustrations on this page show the front and back of an ordinary iron (above and top left), the head of an offset iron (right) and that of a standard metal wood (top right). Familiarize yourself with the names of the different parts of the club heads.

REMEMBER
OFFSET HEADS HELP CURE A SLICE

The Clubs to Suit You

Your choice of clubs is vital. They should be right for your height, strength and general game. In this area it is useful to ask a woman professional for advice.

In theory, most players can use clubs of fairly standard length. Although people's height varies enormously, hands hang at about the same distance from the ground. Women between 1.5m (5ft) and 1.6m (5ft 6in) can normally use standard length clubs.

If you add length to the club, the shaft becomes whippier and the head feels heavier. If you shorten a club, it becomes stiffer and there is usually less feel to the head. Smaller women golfers are best advised not to have their clubs shortened for this reason. It is easier just to grip further down the club.

For tall women golfers, the danger comes from using men's clubs when you haven't the strength. If you are tempted to use men's clubs, ensure you look at those which are really light. A male professional may not help you with this. Women's clubs will feel light to any man and he may find it difficult to distinguish between one set and another.

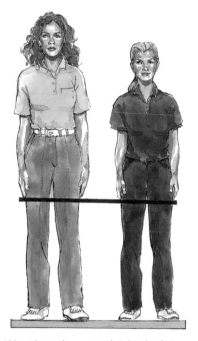

Although people vary greatly in height, their arms tend to hang to about the same distance from the ground, as shown in the illustration above. This means that golf clubs of a standard length will generally suit a golfer of any given height.

➤ It is essential to have the correct lie of clubs – in other words, the angle at which the clubs sit to the ground. As you hit the ball, the shaft flexes, and the hands usually rise slightly through impact. The correct lie of the club should allow you to put a small coin under the toe of the club.

➤ If the player is short or holds her hands low at address, the toe may be off the ground. The tendency is for the heel to drag into the ground and the club face to close. As a result, the shot is pulled or drawn to the left. In other words, the club is too upright. If you are not very tall and you constantly pull shots to the left, this may be the cause.

➤ An incorrect lie to the club is more of a problem for a tall player. The toe may dig in the ground through impact and can cause a chronic slice. Look at the shape of your divot and the mark on the sole of the club to see if this happens. If you are tall, always buy your set of clubs from a professional and make sure they are set up correctly for you. Preferably buy a set which can be altered, but remember that woods cannot generally be altered, so buy these correctly in the first place.

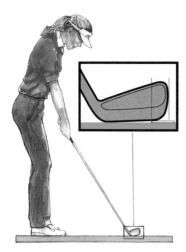

If you select clubs with an incorrect 'lie' to the ground, you are more likely to make errors in your shots. The correct lie – the way the club head 'sits' on the ground – should just enable you to slide a coin under the toe of the club, as shown above.

Taller players need to be closer to the ball than shorter players.

The grips of clubs can have a remarkably pronounced effect on your shots. Ensure you select clubs with the right grip for you and then have them replaced when they begin to wear out.

The shapes of clubs' soles vary according to the number of club and the make. Beginners generally find round-soled clubs (above, right) more forgiving and easier to play with.

➤ Buy clubs with the correct thickness of grip. In theory a thick grip encourages a slice to the right and a grip which is too thin will encourage you to hold the club too tightly or to hook to the left. With the correct grip the fingers of the left hand just barely touch the pad of the left thumb without digging in.

➤ Make sure grips are put on correctly with any line or mark perfectly square to the club face. Grips are generally not perfectly round, but egg-shaped. If incorrectly fitted, you may find difficulty in holding the club face square and returning it squarely to the ball.

➤ Lighter clubs are generally easier to control. The club may feel the correct weight in the pro's shop, but remember that in order for you to be comfortable it still needs to feel light enough by the end of your round.

➤ A round-soled club is more adaptable to different slopes and easier to play with than one with a flat sole.

REMEMBER STIFF SHAFTS LEAD TO POOR SHOTS

What Else Do I Need?

There is a wide range of equipment available. It doesn't
need to be expensive, but it should be chosen with
suitability for your game in mind.

Gloves. Most professional golfers wear a
glove on their left hand – it helps to ensure a
good, consistent grip. It should feel much
tighter than a normal fashion glove, fitting
well on your fingers and thumb. When trying
on a glove, push it down between your
fingers and make sure that the Velcro
fastening pulls across the back of your hand.

Some women golfers also like to wear a
right hand glove. This is more to protect your
hands than to help your grip. If you only
wear a right hand glove in the winter,
remember that the addition of a second glove
can change the way you hold the club. In
effect it makes the grip of the club thicker
and harder to unite your hands.

Leather gloves tend to be more expensive
and usually don't wear as well, particularly if
the weather is hot and your hands perspire.
Synthetic, all-weather gloves come in a wider
range of colours and are usually washable. If
you wash them, do remember to do up the
Velcro first!

In cold weather it is often better to use
sheepskin mittens over your golf gloves and
remove them for each shot. Playing in winter
gloves can again make your grip feel awkward.

Golf balls. The golf ball used by most men
professionals is unsuitable for most women
club golfers. Find a make of golf ball you like
and stick with it.

There are many makes, some with soft
covers and some with harder covers. Soft-
covered golf balls tend to produce more
backspin, more sidespin and tend to lose
distance. Choose a ball with a tough cover,
but an 80 or 90 compression. Too hard a ball
is often difficult for high handicap women
golfers to use. On a 9 metre (10 yard) putt a

soft ball, as used by most professionals, can
run up to a metre (1 yard) shorter than one
more suited to amateur golfers.

Tees. Most professional golfers use wooden
tees, but it is better for most club golfers to
use set-height, 'castle' tees. The advantage of
these is that they encourage you to tee the
ball to the correct height each time. They are
also easier to use when the ground is hard in
the summer, or in winter frost.

Castle tees come in a range of lengths and
are usually colour coded – white being the
highest and orange the lowest.
• The white tee is suitable for a deep-faced
driver.
• The yellow tee is more suited for a shallower
driver or a deep-faced 3 wood.
• The blue tee is ideal for a fairway wood or
long iron from the tee.
• The red or orange tees are for use on par 3s
with your other irons.

Shoes. The most comfortable golf shoes have
leather uppers, which breathe well, but
rubber soles that are flexible. Whether or not
you have shoes with metal spikes, soft spikes
or a built-in rubber sole, ensure that the sole
is sufficiently flexible. If the sole is stiff –
usually leather – the shoe may not bend and
may finish up rubbing your heels.

Shoes can affect your balance. A shoe
with a small heel will push your weight
slightly on to the balls of your feet. A shoe
with no heel at all will push your weight on
to your heels. It is important to find the type
that suits you best. In wet weather you
should have waterproof leather or synthetic
waterproof shoes. As rain can creep in
through the laces, a shoe with a flap is
more likely to keep your feet dry.

Novices should note that training shoes (trainers) are not acceptable at most clubs. **Golf bags.** A beginner usually needs to have a bag which you can use on a trolley and can also carry. It should have a good strap, which is adjustable to allow you to balance it properly. If you use clubs with graphite shafts, ensure that the top of the bag has a soft lining and is graphite friendly. Make sure the bag has a hood that can be fitted easily in wet weather to keep the clubs dry, but allow you quick access. Some bags have dividing tubes, designed to keep the clubs from damaging each other's grips.

The bag you choose should have a section for carrying an umbrella, hooking on a towel and keeping your car keys and valuables safe.

If you carry a bag, try one with a double strap, which is easier on your back and shoulders. As a beginner, learn to carry it correctly – over your left shoulder, not upright, but across your back. Push your left elbow down on the heads of the clubs until the bag lies across the small of your back and feels well balanced.

The choice of golf equipment now available is endless. Go for what is most practical and best suits your pocket.

REMEMBER
GET USED TO
ONE MAKE
OF BALL

The Complete Golfing Kit

Here are details of other golfing equipment which will always come in handy on the course and when you are preparing for your game.

Trolley. If you use a trolley, buy one with an adjustable handle so that you can balance it at a comfortable height. Many trolleys are designed for men who are 2 metres (6ft 6in) tall and not women who are 30cm (1ft) shorter. Check the balance with a set of clubs on it.

Club covers. All professional golfers use covers on their woods, even though the woods are now made of metal. They protect them. A long cover will also protect the shaft of a graphite-shafted wood and stop it banging against the heads of your irons. Very few professional golfers use covers on their irons. They don't need protection and taking covers on and off simply slows up play.

Putter cover. If you have a brass-headed putter or one with a painted finish, then certainly a putter cover will add to the protection of your club.

Electric trolley. If you use an electric trolley, choose one with three wheels and one you push in front of you rather than pull behind you. If you are a senior golfer, make sure you can handle the trolley and load it in your car with ease – the battery can be heavy and the trolley can be a problem to dismantle.

Flight bag. If you travel overseas, a flight bag is a must. Taking golf bags on aeroplanes, tying the clubs together with string and hoping they won't fall out, is not a good idea! You can put your whole golf bag in a flight bag, together with waterproofs, a pair of shoes and all your other accessories.

Practice bag. On the assumption that you are going to practise, make it as easy as possible and have a good practice bag. The ideal type will sit open when you unzip it. With a little skill you will learn to flick balls up with your sand wedge and land them in the open bag. A practice bag that holds 60 balls is plenty – if you have more your practice is likely to become careless. Some players prefer to use a practice tube of just 20 balls. You can also buy a practice ball bag with a built-in tube. This way you don't have to bend down and pick the balls up but can simply stab them. Don't do this on the green. It tends to damage it.

Pitch repairer, rubber sucker and ball marker. You will learn how to repair pitch marks on a green. If you are a high handicap golfer your ball probably won't make a pitch mark, but you will find yourself having to repair other people's as you arrive at the green. Alternatively you can use a tee peg.

Most professional golfers mark the ball on the green with a simple coin. You may prefer a plastic or brass one which may show up better. Most gloves have a small ball marker included in them.

Score counter. If you are a beginner, then you may feel this is essential. You can click forward the score with each shot you hit. Hopefully you soon learn to discard this and will count your shots with ease!

Winter tees. Some golfers like to use a set of three rubber tees, attached together with string. They feel this is easier when the ground is hard – either frosty in winter or baked in the middle of the summer.

There are all sorts of other items available to help you with your golf. These range from towels, ball cleaners, gadgets to hang your putter outside the golf bag, pens or pencils attached to springs, brooches with ball markers attached, gadgets for the end of your putter to hold a ball marker and booklets for keeping your scorecard and pencil dry.

Visit your local golf club's professional's shop to view
the wide range of ancillary golfing kit now available.

REMEMBER
GOLFING
GADGETS
ARE FUN

First Lessons

No woman should ever be tempted to start golf without lessons. Even if you are a gifted games player, you can easily get into bad habits that are difficult to break. Lessons with a professional will ensure you know what you should do from the very start. If you can find a woman professional to go to, even better – she will work systematically through the basic techniques. She will know instinctively what to watch for.

Women are generally more comfortable learning in groups. Newcomers to the game can find it daunting having a professional standing over them for 30 minutes or an hour. It helps to remember that everybody misses the ball repeatedly in their first two or three lessons. If you are having a lesson on your own, you might imagine that you are the first person your professional has ever seen miss the ball! You can feel horribly stupid. In a group lesson, however, what is daunting on your own can be fun. You realize everyone else has the same problems.

Good group teachers will always keep a watchful eye on everyone taking part, steadily adding pieces of information and bringing you on together with a relaxed style. Ideally, you should have a course of 20 group lessons, which will cover everything from putting to driving, and provide plenty of help on how to proceed on the golf course.

A residential school of three, four or five days is the perfect way to start. Learning on a concentrated course, with other like-minded people, can have marvellous results. You don't have a chance to learn bad habits.

If possible, find a professional golfer who teaches with a video camera. When you see yourself in action it is much easier to correct any faults.

Trish Johnson of Great Britain lines up a putt at the Weetabix Women's British Open at Sunningdale, England.

The Grip

How you hold your clubs is all-important to your game. Your grip controls the height, distance and direction of your shots and is the same with all the clubs except the putter. A beginner should learn it with a 7 iron.

1 Sit the club squarely on the ground. The leading edge – the front of the bottom of the clubhead – should point directly away from you and be facing the target. Any line or mark on the grip is directly down the front. Just steady the top of the club with your right thumb and index finger.

2 Hang your left hand loosely down to the side of the club shaft, with the fingertips pointing directly downwards.

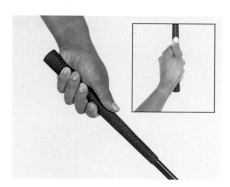

3 Fold the left hand so the thumb and fingers take hold of the club. Now take the right hand away. The club should sit diagonally on the fingers of your left hand with your thumb resting slightly down the right side – it should not feel stretched. The inset picture shows how your left hand should look on the club as you hold it up in front of you – with the thumb slightly down the right-hand side.

4 Lift the club out in front of you and look for these guidelines. The line (or V) between the thumb and index finger should point up towards your right ear or shoulder, not your chin. If you wear a glove you should see part of the logo on the glove. If you don't wear a glove, expect to see two or three knuckles – not one, not all four. With the hand folded over correctly, the fingertips shouldn't be visible.

5 With the club still in front of you, place your right hand so the club sits on the middle joints or tips of all four fingers. Fold the right hand over to complete your grip.

6 The left thumb fits snugly into the palm of the right hand. The right index finger is 'triggered' away from the second finger with a definite gap between the two. The thumb is not straight down the front of the club. The thumb and index finger are split apart with the thumb down the left side of the club. The V between the thumb and index finger should point between the right ear and right shoulder.

7 The powerful trigger position of the right index finger. The tip of the finger hardly touches the club. You want the power in the finger facing the target and not pulling away from it.

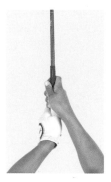

8 CHECK Hold the club up in front of you. In a good grip the hands look elegant. The right index finger is beneath and beyond the thumb. Ensure the clubface is square. Golf grips are not perfectly round but slightly egg-shaped. You should feel a slight ridge in your fingers. Close your eyes, turn the club and feel how you can keep the club square even without looking at the clubface.

COMMON GRIP FAULT

This is probably the most common grip fault, with the index finger pulled up and the thumb down the front. It feels secure but the power is wrongly going up and down rather than towards your target. This position restricts the followthrough and reduces your power.

REMEMBER THE GRIP CONTROLS DIRECTION & DISTANCE

Which is the Grip for You?

You have a variety of grips to choose from. The one that suits you best will take into account the size and strength of your hands as well as the length of your fingers.

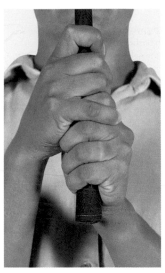

2 The Vardon grip is generally considered to be the perfect and most orthodox one – it is used by most professionals. The little finger of the right hand fits between the first and second finger of the left hand. It pulls the hands together and unites them.

NOTE The conventional Vardon grip may not be right for you if your little finger is very small. Many men have a little finger almost the same length as their third finger, which makes it easier for them.

1 The basic grip (pp. 24–5) is the 'baseball' grip, in which all eight fingers and both thumbs are on the club. It is ideal if you have small hands and can be the easiest one to learn with in the first couple of lessons. However, it has some drawbacks: the hands can easily get out of position and can slip apart if your palms are sweaty or you are undisciplined!

3 The finger spread needed for a perfect Vardon grip. The index finger is spread away for its trigger position and the little finger must easily separate from the third finger. If you start golf as a child this can be easy. If you start as an adult this spread can prove impossible.

4 The 'piggyback' is a version of the Vardon grip which can be easier and is just as good. The little finger of the right hand just sits on top of the index finger of the left and doesn't require the same spread. Remember that the little finger doesn't really do anything. Just relax it and sit it on the outside wherever it feels comfortable. Don't struggle to put it in a specific position.

5 The interlocking grip is often taught to complete beginners, but beware of it. The tips of the left index finger and right little finger are linked, locking the hands together and allowing less movement. For women it is generally a very poor grip because it takes the left index finger off the club, which reduces the strength of the left hand quite dramatically. Women need all the left hand strength they can achieve. Even a left-hander playing golf right-handed might not find the interlocking grip satisfactory.

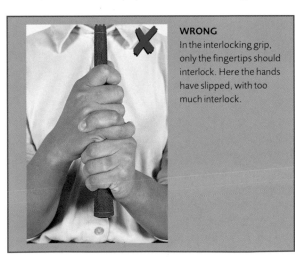

WRONG
In the interlocking grip, only the fingertips should interlock. Here the hands have slipped, with too much interlock.

REMEMBER
OVERLAP FOR
MAXIMUM
POWER

More About the Grip

The way you hold your clubs really does control distance, direction and height. Here are some of the errors that you are most likely to make and how to avoid or correct them.

The 'weak' grip is one where the line or V between the thumb and index finger of one or both hands points up to the chin instead of towards the right shoulder. Caused by the left hand not being sufficiently over the club, the left thumb is too straight on the club and the logo on the glove isn't showing. It can happen if you use an interlocking grip and interlock the whole of the fingers instead of just the tips. This can pull the left hand round to the left.

If you use a weak grip, the result is usually an open clubface through impact – in other words, the clubface facing away to the right with added loft. This allows the ball to slice away with a big bend to the right, being at its worst with a 3 wood or driver.

To correct it, keep the left hand well over and don't interlock.

The 'strong' grip is one where the left hand is too far over and/or the right hand too far underneath. If you are a natural tennis player, your instinct is often to put the right hand under the club with the feeling of scooping the ball into the air. In this position the V between the thumb and index finger of the right hand points far too far outside the right shoulder.

To correct this, sit the club in the fingers of the right hand and *remember*: your right hand must face your target and your target is on the ground down the fairway.

The result of using a strong grip is generally one of closing the face through impact, the clubface facing left with reduced loft. It produces strong shots – hence the name of the grip – but they lack height, particularly when using a driver, 3 wood or 3 iron. This is one of the hardest grip faults to correct. The lower you see the ball fly, the more likely you are to put the right hand under the club. Resist your instinct from racquet sports. You are likely to be at your worst when wanting loft with a sand wedge – so take special care.

The grip should be a finger grip with the thumbs pulled up and not stretched down. The hands should fold and the fingers curl.

To feel a good grip, have someone hold the club towards you. Point your left hand along the club as though shaking hands and fold it over to take up the grip. Then point your right hand along the club, again as though shaking hands, and fold it over. This gives the correct finger grip.

The grip should stay constant from the start to the finish of the swing, although it might loosen slightly at the very end of the followthrough. You need to hold the club firmly in the fingers but with freedom in the wrists. Most men hold a club far too tightly; many women hold too loosely, particularly in the left hand.

To practise keeping a constant grip, line up to a row of four balls. Hit one after another, taking your time, but feeling the grip staying constant from the first ball through to the fourth.

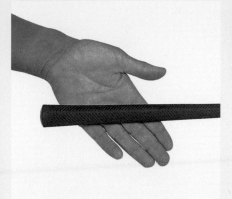

Have someone hold the club towards you. Point your fingers along its grip as though you are shaking hands with the club.

When you close your left hand around the handle of the club, ensure your thumb turns slightly over the right-hand side of the club.

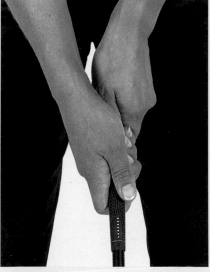

Point your right hand along the club, as though you were shaking hands, and then fold it over your left hand and the club.

CHECK THE GRIP
This is how your grip should look from the front if you have set it up correctly. Check in a mirror that your grip corresponds with the one illustrated in the picture above.

REMEMBER
YOUR RIGHT
HAND SHOULD
FACE THE
TARGET

There are several important elements involved in the way you stand to hit the ball, known to golfers as the 'address position'. You owe it to yourself to get into good habits from the start.

Use a 7 iron. Sit the club squarely on the ground without a ball and hold it lightly with the right hand. Put your feet a comfortable distance apart, say hip width, and bend from your hips, not your waist.

Add your left hand and adjust your right hand to take hold of the club. Your arms should hang reasonably vertically, hands in a direct line below your chin. If you bend correctly, from the hips, your back should feel fairly flat, though not stiff. Your legs should take up a natural flex. Keep your head up and your chin in, with just a natural and comfortable line from the top of your head down your back.

When you can feel the correct posture without a ball, your next move is to adjust your distance from the ball by moving your feet backward or forward. How far you are away depends on your height – shorter people need to stand further from the ball.

Do not 'sit and sag' (see opposite page). This is the typical wrong position. It comes from bending or slouching from the waist, rather than bending from the hips. If you bend wrongly, the legs tend to lock or straighten, after which you are likely to bend them excessively. Unless you are very tall, you hardly need to bend the knees at all. The legs should just feel relaxed.

Keep your head up and your chin in, not poking out. Make your neck feel as long as possible. Your eyes should look down your face.

The posture changes slightly depending on the clubs. The driver is the longest and you should naturally find yourself standing taller with it, your weight slightly back on the heels. With a wedge, the shortest club, you will bend over more, with your weight a little more on the balls of the feet.

ADOPTING POSTURE
Get comfortable, holding the
club lightly in your right hand.

CORRECT POSTURE
Stand reasonably tall and flexed,
but not too stiff.

POSTURE – WOODS

This is the correct posture to adopt when playing a wood. Note how the player is standing tall, with her weight slightly back on her heels.

POSTURE – IRONS

The correct posture with a short iron – in this case a pitching wedge – involves bending over more, with the weight shifting onto the balls of the feet.

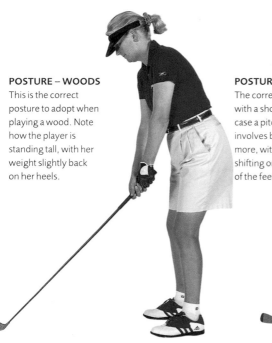

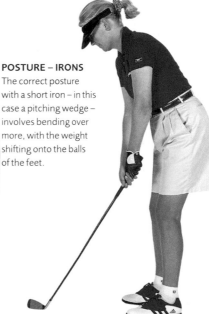

WRONG

Don't listen to a golfing husband who tells you constantly to keep your head down! What he probably means is that you should watch the ball as you hit it. But don't adopt this position or you won't get enough freedom in the swing. NOTE If you wear bifocal glasses, check out other options with your optician as bifocals and playing golf don't mix. With them, you will almost certainly produce this fault.

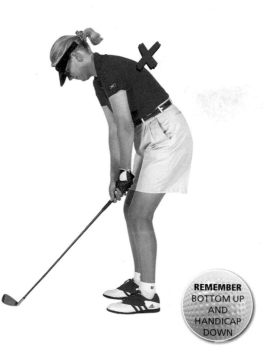

INCORRECT POSTURE

Do not hunch, or 'sit and sag', over the ball as you adopt posture.

REMEMBER
BOTTOM UP AND HANDICAP DOWN

Even professional golfers get in the wrong position from time to time, but you have a greater chance of doing well if you master the basics of a good stance very early on.

Once again, use the 7 iron to practise the basics of adopting the correct stance.

Set your feet so the distance between the outer edge of each is roughly the width of your hips. (Men tend to think in terms of the width of their shoulders; women are better to think in terms of the width of their hips, as these tend to be wider than their shoulders!)

Your right foot should be virtually straight in front, hardly turned out at all, and the left foot should turn out slightly.

With a 7 iron, the ball should be just ahead of centre in the stance. The arms and club shaft should form a natural Y shape.

The right hand is below the left on the club and this will naturally pull the right shoulder slightly below the left.

The left side of the body from hip to shoulder is slightly stretched and the right side of the body slightly relaxed.

Look at the back of the ball – the part you are going to hit – so that your head may tip slightly to the right. Don't exaggerate this.

In the backswing the left arm stays straight and the right folds. They should adopt this position at address. Make sure your left arm sits over your bust and not round to the side of your body. This will start giving you the feeling of the distance you need to be from the ball.

The correct width of stance should allow you to bring your knees together at the end of the followthrough. If your feet are too wide apart you can't achieve this. Nor can you if you wrongly turn the right foot out. Adjust the width of your stance until you easily get a knee to knee position.

With the medium irons – from 5 to 9 – the ball is played just ahead of centre in the

stance. The bottom of your swing should naturally fall at this point and easily collect the ball for a good contact.

With the ball teed up for a drive, or sitting up on a tuft of grass on the fairway, you want to make an upward contact, in order to maximize the advantage of the raised position

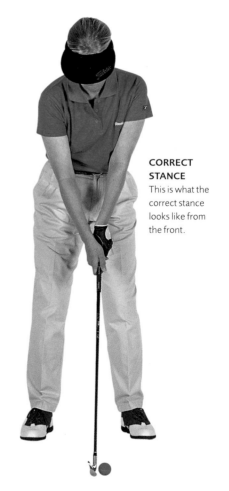

CORRECT STANCE
This is what the correct stance looks like from the front.

of the ball. To encourage this, the ball should be positioned slightly further forward in the stance.

For recovery shots from thick grass, from downhill lies, or for certain shots with a 9 iron or wedge, you want to ensure a downward attack on the ball. You should aim to hit the ball first and the ground after, taking a divot. In these cases the ball should be played further back in the stance, just behind centre, to encourage the downward attack you are looking for.

WRONG
One of the commonest address faults for club golfers is turning the right foot out. It makes the backswing feel easy, but won't allow you to use your feet properly and achieve a good followthrough.

WRONG
Don't push your hands forward excessively. Forget any advice about keeping a straight line down the left arm and the club shaft – though this does apply in some recovery shots. Basically, top women golfers usually form a Y shape at address. Golfing husbands who urge you to push your hands forward aren't helping!

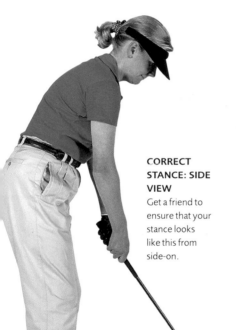

CORRECT STANCE: SIDE VIEW
Get a friend to ensure that your stance looks like this from side-on.

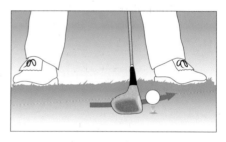

RAISED/UPWARD CONTACT
When the ball is raised, on a tee or tuft of grass, adjust your ball forwards to ensure an upward contact.

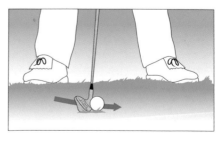

DOWNWARD CONTACT
Position the ball further back in the stance for a downward attack on an awkward lie.

REMEMBER
LEFT FOOT OUT, RIGHT FOOT STRAIGHT

Address – Aiming

The most common error of women golfers is unquestionably aiming away to the right. Spend plenty of time practising your aiming. You can do this in the garden if necessary, without even hitting a ball.

The orthodox address position is known as a 'square' stance. This means you stand parallel to the direction of the shot. In the correct position the lines across the toes, knees, hips and shoulders are all parallel to your shot. The right hand is below the left on the club; it can easily pull the right shoulder forward. The right shoulder should feel down and back, not up and forward. The majority of women golfers have an aiming problem, tending to aim away to the right. If you aim to the right you find yourself hitting some shots away to the right, but you are more likely to turn and pull the ball left of the target. The more you pull the ball left, the more likely you are to aim away to the right.

To aim correctly, stand behind the ball and choose a spot on the ground about 45cm (18in) ahead of it. Go round to address the ball, setting the clubhead as though hitting over the spot. Put your feet together to form a right angle and then put them apart, just

SQUARE STANCE
The square stance is the orthodox position to adopt when addressing the ball. Too often women golfers aim to the right – it is the most common fault in the women's game – but line up squarely and you will hit straighter shots.

CORRECT LINING UP
If you hit a shot to the right, learn to hold your finish and replace your right foot to its starting point. Then lay a club along your toes and check your alignment. The line of the club across your toes should be parallel to the line of flight, not pointing to the target.

thinking of being parallel to the line from the ball over that spot. You are far more likely to aim straight by aiming over a spot than looking at a target 150 metres (165 yards) away. Certain positions on the golf course make aiming seem even more difficult. Aiming from the right side of the fairway or from a badly aligned tee can cause problems.

For specialist, advanced shots we use two other stances – the 'open' stance and the 'closed' stance (see below). An open stance is used to put slicespin on the ball, adding backspin and cutspin to the right. If you inadvertently do this, the ball slices away to the right. A closed stance can be used to produce drawspin, with the ball bending to the left.

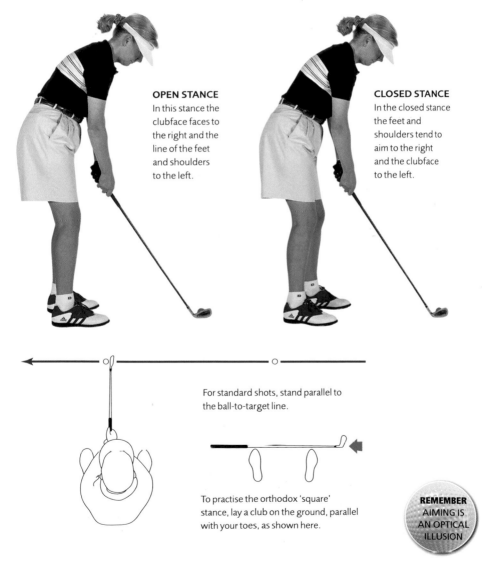

OPEN STANCE
In this stance the clubface faces to the right and the line of the feet and shoulders to the left.

CLOSED STANCE
In the closed stance the feet and shoulders tend to aim to the right and the clubface to the left.

For standard shots, stand parallel to the ball-to-target line.

To practise the orthodox 'square' stance, lay a club on the ground, parallel with your toes, as shown here.

REMEMBER
AIMING IS
AN OPTICAL
ILLUSION

More About the Address

For good players, the most likely faults at address are
having the ball too far forward to the left in the stance
and standing too far away from the ball, particularly
if you are feeling over-confident.

The correct routine should always be to stand
at *approximately* the right distance from the
ball, to set the club down with the right
hand, to adopt the posture and then add the
left hand. Then be prepared to shuffle in or
out towards or away from the ball to find the
correct distance. Find posture first and then
adjust the distance. To check the ball
position, lay one club along your feet,
clubhead round your left foot. Put another at
right angles from the ball to your feet. If you
can't get comfortable at address, set up to the
ball in your normal position. Have someone

else then position another ball slightly further
to the left and another slightly further to the
right. Address these in turn and see if either
feels more comfortable. Try the same exercise
with balls at different distances until you feel
comfortable again.

For advanced golfers searching for
comfort at address, address the ball and
rehearse your backswing. Now address the
ball again, hop the clubhead over the ball
and make a followthrough. Address needs
to feel good, both for going backwards and
for following through.

**POSTURE AND
DISTANCE**
Get yourself into the
correct posture before
adjusting your distance
from the ball. Don't 'sit
and sag' over the ball.
Taller players need to
stand closer to the ball
(far left), shorter players
further away (left).

1 Women golfers need to adjust their distance from the ball so that the left arm lies easily across the bust and not round it. If you get your left arm in the wrong position, you find you have to do a detour in the backswing!

2 If you are of average height – between 1.5m (5ft) and 1.6m (5ft 6in) – here is a good guideline for finding your correct distance from the ball.

For a driver (or, in fact, for most clubs) set your feet level with the grip of the club and the ball at the neck of the clubhead.

If you have problems with the correct distance, make a definite measurement with your driver and your 5 iron so that you can return to it. Measure it with a metre ruler, if necessary, so that you have something to refer to.

3 You can't always see the ball position in relation to your feet. If the ball is too far to the left in the stance, it is particularly likely to occur with a driver or longer club. If you play the ball too far forward, the right shoulder tends to be pulled forward instead of hanging down and the swing becomes difficult. With the ball too far forward, you are likely to pull the ball left or hit the ground behind the ball.

WRONG
Don't plant your feet and then bend over to the ball. It is likely to result in poor posture.

REMEMBER
SWING ERRORS
START AT
ADDRESS

The Simple Swing

The basic golf swing is so simple that a child of eight can do it. Ironically, most adults can't! Young children have no inhibitions and learn by copying – something for novice women golfers to remember.

Adopt a good address position, feeling comfortably tall and relaxed. All the basic learning should be done with a 7 iron. Ensure that your left thumb sits slightly down the right side of the grip. Focus your attention on the left thumb. Turn your back slightly towards the target and lift the club with the arms, supporting it on your left thumb. Stay looking down at the grass.

Swish the club through, brushing the grass at your starting point. Feel the club bouncing on the ground or brushing the grass and don't be afraid of damaging it – or yourself! Don't try the swing with a ball until you can comfortably keep brushing the grass in roughly the right position. Once you can achieve this successfully, perch the ball about 1.5cm (¾in) off the ground on a tee peg and

try the same thing. Don't be surprised if you miss the ball first time. Get confident at hitting the ball from a tee peg. Don't try with it on the ground before you can cope with it on a tee. Practise hitting tee pegs in the garden – just up on the left thumb and through on the left shoulder.

Swish the club through and land it safely on your left shoulder, somewhere between the left shoulder joint and your neck. At this point your right knee should be round against your left leg and the right foot round on the tips of the toes. Just repeat the movement backwards and forwards, backwards and forwards. Gradually learn the feeling of brushing the grass and start trying to feel that you brush the grass at the spot you mean to. Develop freedom in the movement and see it as a simple swing.

SIMPLE SWING EXERCISE
To feel the rhythm of the swing, turn your body to the right and to the left and combine this with swinging the arms up, down, up. Add the club and you can feel the simple swing taking shape.

1 **Address**
At address, you should be standing tall and relaxed, with the arms and club hanging in a Y shape.

2 **Takeaway**
Make sure the toe of your club is pointing upwards at takeaway.

3 **Top of the backswing**
Your back should be facing the target and the club supported on your left thumb.

4 **Impact**
Good impact is all about brushing the grass and ball at exactly the right spot.

5 **Throughswing**
The toe of the club should be pointing upwards, matching the takeaway.

6 **Followthrough**
Your body should be facing the target, with the club shaft settled neatly on your left shoulder.

5   6

EXPERT TIP
Keep practising the swing again and again, up on the left thumb and through on the left shoulder. Gradually turn your body, keeping your back to the target in the backswing – without overdoing it. Turn your body through to face the target in the followthrough, right knee round against the left leg and the club on the shoulder.

REMEMBER
LEFT THUMB, LEFT SHOULDER

Starting at the Finish

There are two stationary positions in the golf swing, the start and the finish which, in golfing terms, are known as the address and the followthrough. A good finish is very important to the swing as a whole.

You should think of the followthrough as being like the brakes on your car: you won't generate speed without a good braking system. When you can get a good start and a good finish, you can then pay attention to your backswing and other parts of the swing, but with an instinct to hit the ball solidly towards your target. Too many golfers spend time thinking about their backswing and forget that the whole idea is to hit the ball to a target that is ahead of you.

Whatever your standard as a golfer, the most important point to remember is: **Think B for Balance**.

CORRECT FINISH
Too many golfers underestimate the importance of achieving a correct finish to the swing in order to make their best shots. The illustrations to the left show the correct position you should achieve at the end of your followthrough, both from the front and the rear. Practise the finish before concentrating on other parts of your swing, and have a friend make sure that you always follow through to the correct finishing position.

RIGHT AND WRONG FINISH
These two illustrations
graphically demonstrate from the
side view how you should and
should not finish your swing. The
correct followthrough should feel
smooth and comfortable, ending
with the club resting on your left
shoulder (left). If you hit yourself
in the face or get your arms
tangled up (right), you are
finishing incorrectly.

In the correct followthrough, your weight should move round towards the left heel with the left leg reasonably straight. The right knee should settle against the side of the left leg with the right foot round on the very tips of the toes. Remember that the right foot has to be straight in front at address to allow this to happen. Your hips should face the target with the weight comfortably set on the left leg.

The club should settle on your left shoulder. If you look down at the club shaft there is usually a label (on a steel) or writing (on a graphite) shaft about 10cm (4in) down from the bottom of the grip. This spot should land comfortably on your shoulder. Don't strangle yourself. The elbows should be level with each other and level with the shoulders, forming a natural right angle. With the wrists released and relaxed the club shaft settles on your shoulder, hands beside your left ear.

CHECK The elbows stay roughly the same width as they started and level with each other. The impression should be of the knees, hips, shoulders and elbows all facing the target. The shoulders will aim slightly left of target but the feeling should be of facing where you are going.

Continue to practise the followthrough without a backswing. Start at address and move through to the finish until you can comfortably settle the club on your shoulder. Remember that you want the club travelling at 160kph (100mph) through impact. You need to learn how to put the brakes on.

At the end of the followthrough, you shouldn't look as though you are going to break your nose or knock yourself out! (See the illustration, above, marked with the cross.) If your followthrough is poor, you won't generate speed. To feel the correct finish, face forward, standing upright, and simply fold your arms up to settle the club on your left shoulder.

Now turn in the feet and legs till you face your target. At the end of the swing you should be balanced on your left leg and you should be able to wiggle the toes of your left foot.

REMEMBER
BE BALANCED
AND THINK
FORWARDS!

The Backswing

Inevitably most of your early lessons on the swing will focus on the backswing. Make sure you don't work so hard on the backswing that you forget that it is simply preparation for hitting the ball forwards.

CORRECT BACKSWING
Aim to emulate the smoothness and stability in the backswing shown here. Note the positions of the arms and feet – left foot bending, back turned towards the target.

The address position prepares you for the backswing. The left arm is straight though not stiff and the right is relaxed. The left shoulder is slightly up and the right shoulder is down and relaxed. The knees are very slightly flexed and knocked in towards each other. The eyes focus on the back of the ball, with the head if anything behind it.

At the top of the backswing, your back has turned to the target with your left arm

swinging across and upwards, supporting the club on the left thumb. The hips and legs move just enough to let this happen. The right leg should stay slightly flexed, not locking and straightening. The club shaft should be horizontal or just above the horizontal. The left arm ideally stays straight, swinging across towards the right shoulder. The right arm should naturally form a right angle.

THE LEFT FOOT

Keep your left foot 'planted' as far as possible throughout the backswing. Lift it a little if it is uncomfortable not to, but never let the foot come all the way up, as shown in the right-hand illustration.

The left arm is straight and is slightly arched, with the right relaxed. In the backswing the left shoulder turns and the left arm swings across the body and upwards, supporting the club on the left thumb. In the perfect position, the back of the left wrist should be almost flat with the club more or less parallel to the line of your shot.

CHECK Your weight starts slightly on the balls of your feet. Professionals often swing to the top of the backswing without lifting the left heel, but most women playing club golf will find they need to. Let the left heel lift slightly, while keeping the ball and toes on the ground. The foot should simply fold and bend as the heel rises up.

WRONG
Don't lift the whole foot without bending it and don't let your little toe off the ground. You have too far to put it back down again by the time you hit the ball.

WRONG
Don't try to keep your left foot flat on the ground if it doesn't feel natural. You may find yourself rolling onto the inside of the foot, which leads to a poor movement as you swing through to impact.

REMEMBER
THE LEFT THUMB SUPPORTS THE CLUB

The Left Arm in the Backswing

Though golf is very much a two-handed game, with
left and right working as one with as even strength as
possible, the harder you make your left arm work in
the backswing the better it will be.

CORRECT TAKEAWAY
The right takeaway
is all-important for
perfecting the
backswing.

TEE PEG EXERCISE
Trap a tee peg
between your
hand and the club
as you swing, to
feel the correct
left-hand contact
with the club in
the backswing.

1 The beginner needs to develop the correct
takeaway in order to produce a perfect backswing.
Swing the club to hip height. The back of the left hand
should face forward and the toe of the club directly
upward. Feel your left thumb on top of the club. I linge
up on the left thumb to form the backswing.

2 CHECK The club should be supported on the
left thumb at the top of the backswing. The grip
should be constant, with the left hand in control
without opening. For a useful exercise, trap a tee peg
between the club and your hand and keep it there
throughout the swing (see illustration above).

LEFT ARM PRACTICE

Swing the club to and fro with only your left arm, as shown here, to get used to feeling your left arm really working in the swing.

PRACTISE THESE SIMPLE EXERCISES

The left thumb should be slightly down the side of the club. From here feel yourself swing the club round and onto the left thumb.

Balance the club between the left index finger and the pad of your hand.

Practise holding the club in your left hand only and swinging it across your body and up to the top of the backswing (above). Then swing it back down slowly but no further than your starting position. Twenty left-handed swings a day works wonders. Remember to keep breathing!

Hold your left arm out in front of you, palm down, with your right hand holding your left elbow. Pull the left arm across your body to your right shoulder. Repeat this until you feel freedom in the shoulder.

At the top of the backswing the left shoulder turns, rounding in towards the right one. This is very different from opening and turning the right shoulder away. This error usually produces an unwanted 'flying' right elbow. Think of your backswing as being dominated by turning the left shoulder, swinging the left arm and supporting the club on the left thumb.

WRONG

The typical fault of women beginners is to allow the clubface to look downward – a shut face as it is known – in the takeaway.

WRONG

From the incorrect takeaway, the left wrist flops over at the top of the backswing instead of the thumb supporting the club as can be seen in the illustration below.

REMEMBER
MAKE YOUR LEFT ARM WORK!

Perfecting the Backswing

The backswing is a turn of the body and a lift of the arms. Try to make it one smooth movement. The simpler you make it, the more you can focus on striking the ball to the target.

TAKEAWAY
As you start to turn in your takeaway, the club should turn with you, its face always square to you.

WRIST HINGING The wrists will naturally hinge and cock upwards as you approach the top of your backswing. Let it happen naturally.

To start the backswing, everything should ideally work together. However, every golfer usually needs a little movement of some sort to get started. Most professionals just make a slight kick forwards with the right knee, which then acts as a trigger for everything to start back in unison.

Don't let your trigger movement be a little forward press with the hands. This can cause problems. Worse still, but very common, is to let the fingers of the right hand open and close and the grip alter as your way of saying 'ready, steady, go'. It's much better to stick to that little right knee movement and set everything off together.

At address, the club shaft should point to your navel – maybe up or down a bit. The clubface faces you. As you start to turn, the club should turn with you with its face always square to you. As it gets to about hip height both wrists should naturally hinge and cock upwards.

You shouldn't feel the wrists hinge. If you make the left thumb support the club and keep the grip constant, it happens naturally.

HEAD RIGHT
This is the correct position for the head at the top of the backswing – just moving slightly to allow the shoulders to turn.

HEAD WRONG
In this illustration the head is in the wrong position – 'staring' too much over the left shoulder. There is not enough room for comfortable shoulder movement here.

You'll notice that better golfers make a little waggle of the clubhead before they commence their backswing. This is simply a way of loosening the wrists slightly. If you learn to waggle the club backwards and forwards before your takeaway, it helps to achieve a perfect backswing where the back of the left wrist is flat. This is the position we aim for with advanced and championship golfers.

Of course, you need to be confident that you aren't going to touch the ball accidentally as you return from the waggle.

As you turn in the backswing, your head must move very slightly to the right to allow your shoulders to turn.

If you keep your head too still you can restrict the backswing. Give yourself just enough freedom, letting it move an inch or so. If you find you have this fault, think of 'right ear down' in the backswing!

At the top of the backswing the shoulders should be more or less horizontal with the left arm always lifted above the shoulders.

REMEMBER
LOOK AT THE BACK OF THE BALL

Attacking the Ball

Now we come to the important part of the swing – making contact with the ball. A good backswing prepares you for this, creating potential power.

ADDRESS AND IMPACT

Think of your address position and your strike position as one and the same thing. Essentially you want to return through your address position at the point of impact, so although the position of things will inevitably change slightly, aim to do just that.

1

2

1 The address position rehearses the impact position. The hips and legs will always be in a slightly different position, but if you think of the address as rehearsing your strike, it keeps your brain moving forwards!

2 At the top of the backswing your back is turned towards the target, the arms lift and the left thumb supports the club. The hips and legs turn enough to allow this to happen. The left heel may or may not lift – it doesn't matter.

3 To start the downswing, push your weight firmly back towards your left heel. If the heel was off the ground at the top of the backswing, get

it firmly back onto the ground – and keep it there. NOTE For low handicappers the correct weight transfer feels *round* towards the left heel, not just sideways to the target. But in doing it, the hips mustn't become too active.

The left arm should work hard to start the downswing, pulling down and away from the right shoulder. The left arm swings to the right shoulder in the backswing and away from it to start the downswing.

4 With the left arm in control, and the right shoulder passive, the club attacks the ball in a curved path, producing an impact position as similar to address as possible, and on into the followthrough.

3

4

COMPLETING THE ATTACK

After the point of impact, make sure you complete the swing properly. No matter how successfully your strike emulated your original address, without a decent followthrough your shot will inevitably fail.

TRY THIS EXERCISE

Address and impact should be virtually the same. To practise this, use an old car tyre and set up to strike it. Swing gently back and through, back and through. Each time you strike the tyre you should feel as though you are just returning to your address.

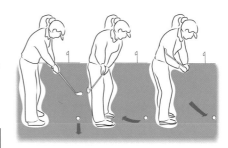

WRONG

At the top of the backswing the right shoulder is in a potentially dominant position. If it turns into the shot too early the attack becomes left-aimed ('out-to-in') and too steep.

BACK AND THROUGH

Do not allow your hips to become too active as you swing back and through in your attack.

REMEMBER
ADDRESS
REHEARSES
IMPACT

Striking the Ball

Most men find striking a golf ball easy. Most women don't. Women beginners tend to be afraid of damaging the ground or themselves, but focus and concentration can build confidence.

Watch the ball at impact. Keep your eyes on the back of the ball – the part you are going to hit. See the ball as you hit it and then see the grass after the ball has gone.

As a beginner have plenty of practice swings, learning to brush the ground exactly where you intend to.

Through impact, the left heel should be firmly on the ground, the eyes stay focused on the back of the ball and the clubhead brushes the ground exactly where the ball sits. The arms should feel stretched because they are travelling fast. All your thoughts are on making a good contact.

Striking the ball is like using a hammer – the hammer moves backwards and forwards on the same curved path. The same should happen with a golf club – the takeaway and attack should follow the same curved path. Imagine you have a nail in the back of the ball and are trying to hit it forward with a long-handled hammer.

In the wrong attack, the clubhead usually moves away on a smooth curve but then attacks the ball too steeply. In terms of our hammer and nail, the hammer would be hitting downwards and bending the nail rather than driving it forwards. The cause for women is usually the right hip, which gets in the way of making a curved attack.

Contact with the ball is all-important. The basic swing with a 7 iron is adapted

PERFECT STRIKE
Watch the ball intently, keep your left foot down and concentrate all your thoughts on making good contact.

depending on the contact you want to make.

With a driver you sweep the ball away on the upswing. The ball is positioned further forward in the stance (see p. 33).

With most iron shots you sweep the ball away with the ball just ahead of centre.

With downhill and recovery shots you make a downward contact, taking the ball and then a little divot.

MAKING CONTACT

There are two dimensions to making a good contact. The first is to judge the depth, striking the ball and just brushing the grass underneath it. The second dimension is learning to strike the ball from the middle of the clubface. Making a good contact is a skill all of its own. You can have the best swing in the world and still make a horrible contact. It is a question of learning to make the club come down where you mean it to.

Hit some shots just thinking of your contact. Give yourself five out of five for a perfect contact down to zero for a bad one. Assess the problem: is your depth wrong? Or are you striking the ball badly?

DRIVING RANGES

A driving range is the ideal place to concentrate on improving your striking of the ball. You can take as many practice swings as you like, hit as many balls as you want, and listen for that elusive perfect contact.

HIT THROUGH THE BALL

Aim at the very back of the ball, imagining there is a nail in it that you want to drive forwards. Hit all the way through the ball at the point of impact, smoothly sweeping the ball away.

TRY THIS EXERCISE

Put a blob of lipstick or chalk on the back of the ball, hit it and see where the mark is left on the clubface. Unless you are a very good player you won't find them all in the middle of the clubface. Just keep looking at the ball, practise more and assess each contact. On a driving range you can hear how well some players contact the ball. Listen for a perfect strike.

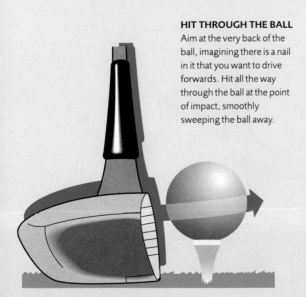

REMEMBER
WATCH THE
BALL!

Followthrough

Many golfers underestimate the importance of the followthrough. It controls both the distance and direction of shots, and consistency of the followthrough is an asset.

You may hear golfers say: 'If I do a good shot, I followthrough.' What they should really be thinking is: 'If I can make myself followthrough, I have far more chance of making a good shot.' Good golf is all about making your best swing more often. Most club golfers vary comparatively little in their address position and backswing, but then

WRONG If your left arm stays too stiff through impact and does not turn, the clubface looks upwards, distance is lost and the shot tends to bend away to the right.

WRONG From the top of the backswing the weight remains on the ball of the left foot. If you do this you will find yourself making a little step forward at the end of the swing.

make a variety of followthroughs at the end of their swings.

Anyone who plays a sport such as tennis will know that you can swing the racquet back the same way time after time and make a variety of shots by altering the way you swing through. In tennis you are trying to surprise an opponent. In golf you want no surprises! Halfway through the throughswing is where you feel direction to the shot. The hands and wrists should turn and swish on through, taking the club through a square – toe up – position (see photographs left and right). The takeaway and throughswing mirror each other. The right arm folds in the backswing and the left arm folds in the followthrough.

For the champion golfer, the left arm is in control and works hard. For the club golfer, it usually needs to relax and get out of the way. The eyes remain focused on where the ball was, seeing the grass after the ball has gone.

By this stage the weight is well round on to the left heel, the right knee is through toward the left leg and the whole body, including the head, starts to turn towards the target.

A good followthrough should give the impression of hitting towards the target. At the end of the swing your knees, hips, shoulders and elbows all face the target. The shoulders will always be slightly left – perhaps 10 degrees. The club shaft settles neatly on your left shoulder, your elbows are roughly the same width apart as they started and are level with each other and level with the shoulders.

The key to good direction is to keep both elbows somewhere in front of you with the club through on your shoulder. You should

be able to see over your right elbow. If you get a hole in one, you should be able to watch it go in!

Balance is crucial. It allows you to generate maximum speed. By the end of the swing your weight is on the left heel with the right foot turned on to the toe of the shoe. You should never feel you are gripping or grabbing with the toes of your left foot. You should be able to wiggle your toes as you would in a normal standing position. Feel the same balance at the end of the swing. Remember that the followthrough is like the brakes on your car. If your followthrough is weak and poorly balanced, you won't generate speed.

At the end of the swing your left leg should be fairly firm and balanced with the left hip naturally out to the side so that your weight is centred over your left leg. This is more noticeable in women than in men; our whole centre of gravity is different.

The golf club should always swing on its own natural angle. The clubshaft at address should fall into the same position in the followthrough. The 7 iron swings up, down, and up. The swing with a wood is naturally flatter.

In a perfect swing the angle of the clubshaft in the followthrough follows the angle of the clubshaft at the address position.

REMEMBER
ELBOWS STAY
CLOSE

Perfecting the Followthrough

If you develop an instinct to finish well, it keeps your
mind focused on striking the ball and making good
shots. If you make a good followthrough it will also
often correct the errors in the backswing.

It is rather like throwing a ball. If you throw a
ball to a target straight in front of you, your
arm swings back in response to this. If you try
to throw the ball to the right, your arm moves
back differently. The thoughts of how you
followthrough with that throw determine how
you swing backwards. The same applies to the
golf swing. Get the attack and followthrough
correct and the backswing falls into place.

There are two points of power in the golf
swing. The first is to deliver power through
impact with maximum speed. The second is
to put the brakes on smoothly at the end of
the swing. Hitting the ball hard doesn't mean
strangling yourself in the followthrough. Feel
the strength and control of your finish.

The aim should always be to release and
relax through impact. You have to get rid of
the power of the swing into the golf ball. You
shouldn't find yourself holding your breath at
the end of the swing. If you are, this is a sure
sign of too much tension, which means you
didn't get rid of all the power into the ball.

To feel a really good followthrough, hit the
ball, hold the finish and count out loud 'one,
two, three, four'. If you are holding your
breath, you can't count! When you first start
doing it, that count of four will probably feel
ridiculously long. For a good woman golfer
the ball should be in the air for about eight
seconds. Holding the followthrough for a
count of four isn't long: it encourages you to
make a followthrough, it ensures you are
perfectly balanced and makes sure that you
breathe properly.

At the end of a perfect followthrough your
legs and shoulders should stay still for several
seconds. The arms unwind first, returning

naturally to the side of your body, elbows still
bent, club shaft pointing up in front. This is the
position almost all professionals hold as they
watch the ball flying towards the flag. If your
followthrough has been good you will easily
come to this position, where the direction of a
good followthrough can clearly be seen.

As an exercise, extend the count of four.
Hold the finish, count one, two, three, four.
Arms down, legs and shoulders still, then count
five, six, seven, eight. It takes eight seconds to
make a hole-in-one! If your swing has been
good the club should naturally return to a
square position and not to an open position.

A woman golfer wants to create as much
speed as she can through impact. If you feel
that you swing too fast, this is usually caused
by poor balance. The better your balance the
more speed you can generate.

RELEASE AND RELAX
You need to concentrate
on getting all your power
into the shot and on into
the followthrough. You
can only do this if you
remain loose and let go.

**PERFECT FINISH
(right)**
Liselotte Neumann of
Sweden holds a perfect
finish during the Trygg
Hansa Ladies Open.

REMEMBER
BALANCE –
ONE, TWO,
THREE,
FOUR

Club Know-How

In theory, the swing with every club should be the same. But for most people the swing with irons and the swing with woods feels different. The irons are shorter and heavier. The woods are longer and lighter. When they start playing golf, many women are initially afraid of a driver or 3 wood because they imagine they are long and heavy. But in fact it is just the opposite – they are lighter.

All the clubs should balance the same. If you think about the maths you learnt at school you realize that the heavier head on a shorter shaft balances in the same way as a lighter head on a longer shaft.

Know the differences

The clubs 'sit' at a different angle from one another. The 7 iron sits up towards you, so that the swing is very much 'up-down-up'. Conversely, the woods sit altogether flatter and out and away from you – encouraging a more rounded swing than that for irons. The beginner usually starts with a 7 iron and then, when moving on to the woods, has to make a conscious effort to make a flatter, much more rounded swing.

Emilee Klein of the USA, with a driver at the Dinah Shore Tournament, Mission Hills Golf Club, USA.

The Short Irons

The 8 iron, 9 iron, pitching wedge and sand wedge are the clubs providing most accuracy when hitting shots into the green. As with any other shot, in each case a good contact is most essential to success.

BALL THEN DIVOT
Take the ball and then a shallow divot, but do not bury your club in the ground!

The diagram on the opposite page shows the relative distances achievable with the short irons by a good amateur woman golfer. Club golfers should aspire to hit these distances.

The contact with a short iron is crucial. You must find the bottom of the ball in order to get good height. A poor contact usually results in shots of poor height and too much length. The ball should be positioned just about centrally in the stance. A top player might be a little ahead of centre and a high handicapper just behind.

The ball position must make you want to hit down through the ball, taking the ball and then the grass just beyond it.

The photograph above shows good contact with a 9 iron. The key to the correct impact is the downward contact on the ball, taking the ball and then the divot. The divot is shallow and the club comes through and out the other side.

Don't bury your club in the ground. Men sometimes do this, and have the strength to. But it produces inaccurate shots and isn't necessary!

If you suffer from a strong grip (see p. 28), when using a short iron you may be tempted to slide the right hand under the club to scoop the ball up into the air. Keep the right hand well over and think of hitting down with the right hand and not up.

SHORT IRON HITTING DISTANCES

8 iron

100–110 metres (110–120 yards)

9 iron

90–100 metres (100–110 yards)

Pitching Wedge

85–90 metres (90–100 yards)

Sand Wedge

35–65 metres (40–70 yards)

The short irons have the most lofted faces of all the clubs in the bag. This means that they will hit higher, shorter shots, to the distances indicated above.

REMEMBER
TAKE A
DIVOT

The Long Irons

The long irons can be difficult even for very good women golfers. They require strong wrists, and accurate contact and steady nerves. A beginner may take time to feel happy with them.

The long irons are those numbered from 1 to 5. For women golfers, and most men for that matter, the 1 and 2 are only for world-class professionals. Many women professionals no longer carry a 3 iron and prefer a 7 wood, which is easier to use and covers the same distance.

The diagram at the bottom of the opposite page shows the distances of the 3 to 5 irons for a good amateur/women club professional. There should be about a 9metre (10 yard) gap between each club, and the further the distance the lower the height of the ball during the shot.

The long irons are longer and lighter than the shorter ones. It can be difficult to feel the clubhead. The ideal contact for a woman golfer is to sweep the ball off the grass without any real divot. It is easy with the heavy head of a 9 iron to take the ball and divot. Most women find this harder with the long irons and it isn't really necessary.

If the lie is good with the ball sitting on a little tuft of grass, position the ball just ahead of centre, watch the ball well and just sweep it away, lightly brushing the grass on which the ball sits. It is harder if the ball sits on a tighter lie with less grass. Try just to sweep the ball away.

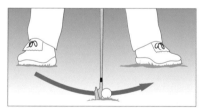

LONG IRON STANCE VERSUS LIE
When you have a good lie, position the ball just ahead of centre in your stance (top). With a tighter lie (below), position the ball further back and hit down.

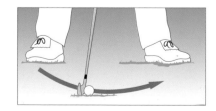

The long irons require good tempo and rhythm. The ball should, of course, travel 27metres (30yards) further with a 4 iron than with your friend, the 7 iron. But don't press for distance. Allow the extra length of the shaft and reduced loft – the angle of the clubhead which affects height – to produce distance. Swing more slowly with the long irons and trust the club to give you the distance.

PLAYING LONG IRONS

When playing a long iron shot, the objective for a woman golfer should be to sweep the ball away off the grass with the minimum of ground contact.

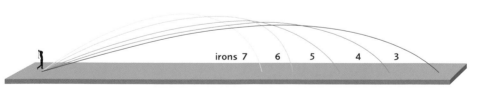

irons 7   6   5   4   3

LONG IRON DISTANCES

Remember – the lower the number of the club you hold in your hand, the further it will hit the ball. The diagram above and distance chart opposite show the distances a good woman golfer could reasonably expect to hit with the different long irons.

7 iron 110–130 metres (120–140 yards)
6 iron 120–140 metres (130–150 yards)
5 iron 130–150 metres (140–160 yards)
4 iron 140–155 metres (150–170 yards)
3 iron 145–160 metres (155–175 yards)
2 iron 150–165 metres (160–180 yards)

REMEMBER
SWING
SLOWLY –
MAINTAIN
RHYTHM

Check Out Your Long Iron Faults

Contact with the ball is at the heart of women golfers' problems with long irons. The lightness of the head can be unforgiving. Later you will see why a fairway wood can be so much easier to use.

When practising your long irons, focus more than anything on your contact. Listen to your strike on the ball. By listening for it you can feel the timing you are trying to produce. You can hear whether the contact is a clean one. Award yourself five points for a perfect contact and zero for a horrible contact and just keep focusing on scoring fours and fives.

If you have a faulty or loosening grip during the swing, it will show up most with the long irons. One of the most typical faults for a woman is to hit the ground behind the ball. If this is your problem, make sure the ball is positioned only just ahead of centre in the stance and keep your left-hand grip firm from address through impact.

The diagram below shows the difference between the 7 wood (left) and the 3 iron (right). They will cover much the same distance. The sole of the 3 iron is narrow and the sole of the 7 wood is wide. If your contact with the 3 iron is less than perfect, the club tends to cut into the ground. Most women lack the strength to take a solid divot. By contrast, the 7 wood has a large, bouncy sole. If you should hit even 2.5cm (1in) or so behind the ball, the sole of the 7 wood simply bounces along the ground and will still make a good contact. It is far more forgiving for the average player.

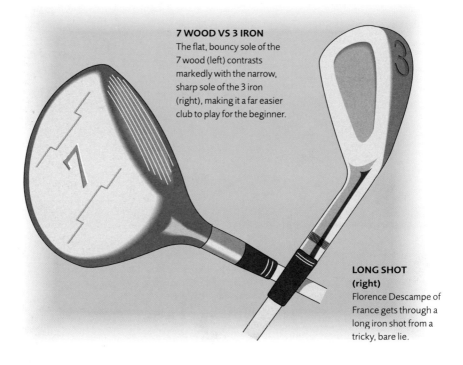

7 WOOD VS 3 IRON
The flat, bouncy sole of the 7 wood (left) contrasts markedly with the narrow, sharp sole of the 3 iron (right), making it a far easier club to play for the beginner.

LONG SHOT (right)
Florence Descampe of France gets through a long iron shot from a tricky, bare lie.

REMEMBER
THE 7 WOOD IS
EASIER THAN
A 3 IRON

The Driver

The driver is the longest but lightest of the clubs and is designed to give maximum distance with tee shots on long holes. The deep head allows you to tee the ball up nice and high to launch it into the air.

Drivers vary in loft from 7degrees to as much as 13 degrees. Men tend to hit the ball higher than most women and their stronger wrists tend to produce greater backspin on their tee shots. The ideal loft of the driver for most women golfers is 12 degrees, which will help a beginner produce plenty of loft and, with this, maximum distance.

A driver with 12-degree loft is quite forgiving. A club with very little loft puts on more sidespin and is more difficult to hit straight. You want a slightly upward contact with the driver. Position the ball ahead of centre in the stance. Tee it up as high as the depth of your clubhead allows (see right).

At address the arms and club shaft form a definite Y shape. Feel the left side of the body slightly stretched and right side relaxed, giving you the feeling of producing an upward contact (see right).

Find a flat place on the teeing ground to tee the ball. Remember you can go backwards up to two club lengths behind the tee box. It is the one place on the course where you can tread down behind the ball – get used to doing so.

Beginners should notice the correct way of teeing up a ball. Hold the ball in the palm of your right hand and the tee peg between the first and second fingers (see diagram opposite). Use the ball to push the tee into the ground. This way it balances easily and you learn to get a consistent height to your peg.

Make sure you sit the clubface squarely with the back of the club on the ground and the full loft showing on the clubface. Don't fall into the common fault of pushing the hands forward and shutting the face downwards.

The swing should be full and rounded, not up and down. With the backswing and throughswing mirroring each other, sweep the ball up and away. Focus on hitting the tee peg out of the ground for good height.

ADDRESS WITH A DRIVER
At the address with a driver, the ball should be positioned forward in the stance, ball teed high to encourage an upward contact.

THE HEAD OF THE DRIVER
Buy a driver with a large head and 11 or 12 degrees of loft, for maximum distance and accuracy.

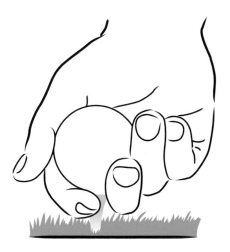

TEEING-UP
Use the ball to push the tee peg into the ground, as shown in the diagram. It is better to use a 'castle' tee peg with a pre-set height until you are confident about setting ordinary tees to a height you are comfortable with.

REMEMBER
HIT THE TEE PEG AWAY WITH THE BALL

Driving for Distance and Direction

Good driving requires sound aiming. Right from the time you tee up, you should be considering the best way of reaching a definite target.

1 The swing with a driver should be rounded, making a powerful horizontal attack into the back of the ball. Remember that the plane of the swing should follow the angle of the club shaft at address.

2 Have the courage to turn away from the ball in the backswing. Make sure that you really do turn your back to the target, rather than simply lifting the arms and club. You want to make a horizontal attack.

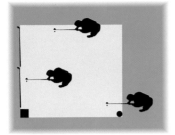

TEE POSITION
Choose your tee position
carefully (left). One side
of the tee may give an easier
view of your target than
the other.

3 Think of the contact with the driver as like striking a nail into the back of the ball. The hammer head (clubhead) should move in a shallow curve both back and through. Don't pick the club up as though bending your nail.

A good way of feeling a shallow takeaway and shallow attack is to hold the club slightly off the ground at address. Many tournament professionals do this – it helps the player make a low takeaway. If by contrast you sit the club directly on the ground, the first movement can easily be one of lifting it.

4 Followthrough for power: If you practise on a driving range, position an upside-down tee peg on the mat about 45cm (18in) behind the ball and about 10cm (4in) toward your feet. The feeling should be of a shallow takeaway, easily collecting that tee peg. The average woman golfer will usually lift her arms, making too steep a takeaway and too steep an attack.

Keep the right shoulder comfortably down at address, the ball just 5–7.5cm (2–3in) ahead of centre in the stance and learn the feeling of a low takeaway and low attack.

REMEMBER
SHALLOW
TAKEAWAY,
SHALLOW
ATTACK

The Fairway Woods

This collection of woods is designed to produce a range of long shots of varying heights and lengths. The fairway woods comprise the 3, 4, 5, 7 and 9 and have different degrees of loft.

The 3 wood gives the longest shots and is comparatively difficult for the average woman golfer. It is more commonly used as an alternative to the driver. A 4 wood is an easier club from the fairway than a 3 wood but is not often made. The standard fairway wood for an average woman golfer is a 5. This should give good height and maximum carry. The 7 wood is then an alternative to a 3 or 4 iron and much easier to hit with. The 9 wood is comparable in distance to a 5 iron. The shafts of all woods are longer than irons, so your posture needs to be more erect and your swing plane slightly flatter.

The sole of a wood is very different from that of an iron. It bounces on the ground while the leading edge of an iron is designed to cut in and take a divot.

For fairway shots it is important to sit the club absolutely flat to the ground to take advantage of the bouncing sole. If you wrongly push your hands forward, the back edge of the club will rise and you will lose the forgiving effect of a wood.

1 At address the clubface must sit squarely and the arms and clubshaft form a natural Y shape. If the lie is very grassy and the ball sits up well, play the ball several inches ahead of centre. If the lie is tighter – with less grass beneath the ball – position it just ahead of centre.

2 The contact is the crux of making good fairway wood shots. The clubhead must bounce on the ground in exactly the right spot. Before any fairway wood shot, always have one or two practice swings and make sure that the front edge does not dig in. You shouldn't really mark the fairway. The contact is rather like striking a match – in and out.

Never try to play a fairway wood without that practice swing. The contact is crucial. Rehearse it as often as you need to. The ball is collected right from the bottom of the swing.

3 The swing is much the same as that for the driver, with emphasis on roundness, but brushing the ground rather than simply picking the ball off the tee.

A 3 wood from a tee is a much better choice for most longer handicap golfers than using a driver. The ball needs to be teed slightly lower to ensure the club head can't pass right under it. The technique is then the same as with the driver, making sure you take the peg and the ball. The added loft of the 3 wood makes it a more forgiving shot.

REMEMBER PRACTICE SWINGS FOR FAIRWAY WOODS

Fairway Woods – Awkward Lies

The fairway woods can also be used from light rough or certain poor lies. However, don't be too greedy. Remember that the heavier head of an iron is generally more suited to getting out of the rough. But if the ball sits well, the 7 wood is a good choice.

Always think carefully about the shot. Keep in mind the saying 'a wood in the rough, means wood in your head!' If you have a poor lie on the fairway, with the ball in a slight divot perhaps, push your hands slightly forward at address. This will lift the back of the clubhead, giving a cutting edge like an iron. In such a situation the face of the club is described as being slightly 'hooded'. In other words, you have lost the loft of the wood and given yourself a club which will respond more like an iron.

When playing from a poor lie with a wood, you can expect the followthrough to be slightly stunted. Punch the ball away more like an iron shot.

If you play a 3 wood well from the fairway, there will be times when the extra length

achievable with this club will stand you in good stead. There are even times when a driver from the fairway can be really useful, but you will need to be very proficient at the game before this is really an option. If you are lucky enough to find your ball sitting on a real tuft of grass – and it does happen occasionally! – you can treat it like a tee shot and use a driver. The contact in this shot does, however, have to be absolutely perfect. Have two or three practice swings, making sure that the bottom of the club really does bounce on the ground at the point of impact. Watch the ball well through impact and trust your driver, hitting the ball with confidence. Such a choice can be particularly useful when you are playing into the wind. The aim is to achieve a low shot with lots of run.

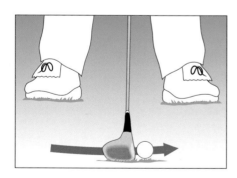

FROM A TIGHT, BARE LIE
The contact you should aim for from a tight lie with little or no grass is to bounce the club on the exact spot on which the ball sits, nipping it up and away. Bounce the sole of the club down and up, in and out, like striking a match.

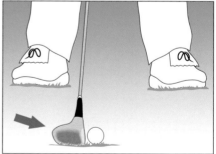

FROM A BAD LIE
Use a 5 or 7 wood from a bad lie. Aim to tip the face of the club over slightly and bring the back of the sole off the ground to get into any slight depression. Hold the shaft and hands slightly forward to the left to achieve a downward attack.

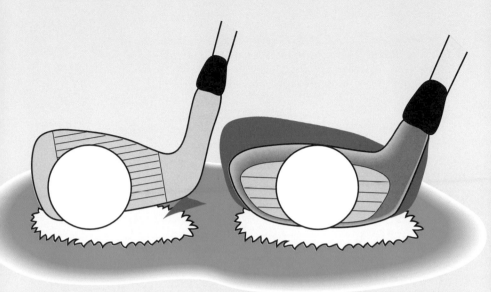

EXPERT TIPS

➤ From a bad lie, never try to help the ball up, whichever club you are using. Let the loft of the club get it up. Move through on to the left foot for a downward attack. Think *down* to squeeze the ball up and away.

➤ With a fairway wood from a tight lie, the main consideration with the shot is good judgement of depth: the tighter the lie, the better your judgement of depth needs to be.

➤ Always take two or three practice swings before playing your shot to ensure that your depth is right. Make sure that the sole of the club bounces on the ground. *Listen* for the clubhead bouncing on the ground.

➤ The worse the lie, the farther back in your stance you should play the ball.

➤ In squeezing the ball out of a poor lie with a fairway wood, aim to take a tiny divot.

GOOD CONTACT OUT OF DIVOT HOLES

To make a good contact with a short pitch out of a divot hole, think of balancing the clubhead toward its toe (above left). This may help you find the bottom of the ball. A small-headed fairway wood (above right) can sometimes be easier than a long iron when playing from a divot.

REMEMBER
HANDS
FORWARD FOR
TROUBLE
SHOTS

Making a good contact is a skill of its own. Women beginners often develop a good-looking swing quickly and easily but have to be taught how to make a perfect contact. The first skill is learning to make good depth, brushing the ground exactly where you mean to.

Topped shots

Topped shots are the most likely bad shot of women beginners. You simply hit the top of the ball and it runs along the ground instead of getting airborne.

In a topped shot, the club strikes the ball at its top or halfway up instead of brushing the ground beneath it.

One of the most common reasons that a topped shot occurs is because you are looking at the ball wrongly. If you wrongly look at the top of the ball you will hit the top of the ball. You shouldn't look at the ball as a whole object. You must focus very definitely on the back of the ball. This doesn't mean putting your head in a funny position but simply focusing your eyes on the back of the ball, to the exclusion of anything else.

Women golfers are also often afraid of brushing the ground. They think it is untidy to take a divot or seem to worry it will hurt. Get used to brushing the ground. You have to remember that the ground gets in the way of every shot you play. You must overcome inhibitions about striking it. Have plenty of practice swings in the garden or on the practice ground and gain the confidence to brush the ground just where you want to.

The main swing fault causing a topped shot is tension. If you become tense or hold your breath during the shot, your whole rib cage lifts and the clubhead no longer gets back down to the ground.

To cure topped shots, think of the contact. Give yourself five points for a perfect contact and zero for a horrible contact. Relax with your arms loose and long, look at the back of the ball and concentrate on brushing the

ground at the right spot. Don't try to help the ball into the air. Trust the loft of the club to get the ball airborne.

'Fat' or 'fluffed' shots

The other depth problem is 'fat' or heavy shots (also called 'fluffed' shots!). These happen when you dig too deep or, more commonly, hit the ground behind the ball. They are often caused by loosening the grip in your fingers, usually at the top of the backswing. When you pull the club back into the fingers the clubhead hits behind the ball.

Check your ball position. The bottom of your swing should be roughly opposite your nose, in other words at the centre of the stance. Make sure the ball is positioned centrally.

If you hit the ground behind the ball you are probably trying to help it into the air, as though playing a racquet shot. You may find you keep your weight on your right foot as though trying to scoop the ball into the air. You should ensure that you transfer your weight properly on to your left foot by the end of the swing. Think down rather than up as you swing through the ball.

CORRECT CONTACT (right)
If you try to lift the ball the clubhead will rise and catch the top (see opposite, top right). In order to counter this, transfer your weight to the left foot through impact. Hit down through the ball, ideally taking a divot, to force the ball up and away, in the opposite of a topped shot.

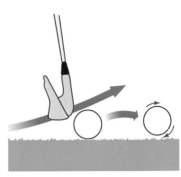

TOPPED SHOTS – POINT OF IMPACT

This diagram demonstrates what happens when you look at the top of the ball and hit there rather than in the back of the ball. The ball is scuffed forward and leaps into a low, weak topspin away.

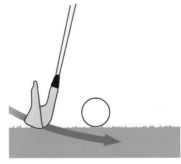

FAT OR FLUFFED SHOTS

In a fat or fluffed shot, the club hits the ground behind the ball. To avoid this, keep the ball fairly central in the stance and aim for a ball then divot contact, with your weight on the left heel through impact.

REMEMBER
GOOD
CONTACT
IS A SKILL

One of the problems for beginners is that they mis-hit the ball and don't understand what is happening. If your contact is poor, you have to try to assess why before finding the cure.

There are two dimensions to making a good contact. One is the depth (when it is not right, topped shots and fat shots result – see pp. 72–3). The other dimension is hitting the ball from the middle of the clubface – middling it, as it is known. If you don't do it correctly, it causes your ball to shoot off low or to right or left, particularly with an iron. To find out if this is a fault, put a blob of lipstick or chalk on the back of the ball and see where it leaves a mark on your club at impact. A shank or 'socket' is the most devastating of shots. The ball comes off the neck and either scuttles along low or shoots off to the right.

Address the ball correctly in the middle of the clubface. The ball position can be an optical illusion. In your address position, the ball may look central on the clubface but if you look at it from behind it is too near the neck. There is plenty of power towards the toe of the club. Address the ball centrally or even towards the toe.

A shank is usually caused by poor balance. Through impact you should be firmly on your left heel. If you wrongly let your weight move toward the toes, the clubhead swings down in the wrong place and almost certainly you find yourself wanting to step forward at the end of the followthrough. Make sure your weight is transferred properly on to the left heel and that the toes of your left foot are free – not gripping or grabbing to keep you balanced.

A shank is more likely to occur if you stand too far from the ball and are being pulled forward off balance than by standing too close to the ball. Even changing your shoes to ones with a slightly higher heel can cause a shank because this can affect your balance in the stance.

Shots from the toe of the club shoot off to the right but with a much softer contact than shanks. Again, if you don't know which you are doing, try the exercise with two balls or the blob of lipstick test to assess it. Shots from the toe are like topped shots and are usually caused by tension and pulling in through impact. Fear is usually at the bottom of the problem. Try to relax.

To cure shots from the toe, practise with a tee peg just outside the ball (see opposite).

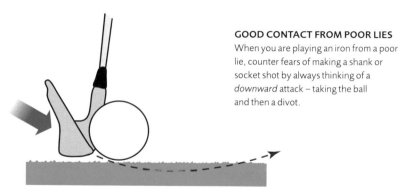

GOOD CONTACT FROM POOR LIES
When you are playing an iron from a poor lie, counter fears of making a shank or socket shot by always thinking of a _downward_ attack – taking the ball and then a divot.

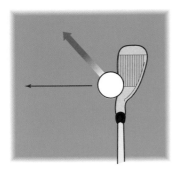

SHANKED SHOTS

A ball hit with the socket will fly sharply off to the right. This is often caused by wrongly addressing the ball in the neck of the club, or bad balance through impact.

CURING THE SOCKET SHOT

Practise getting rid of the socket shot by setting two balls down about 2.5cm (1in) apart and aiming to catch just the nearest one each time. If you hit both balls, then you are still making contact with the socket.

CURING SHOTS FROM THE TOE

Practise placing a tee peg alongside your ball and hitting it away together with the ball. Check your practice swing: brush the ground where you mean to.

REMEMBER BALANCE!

Watching the Ball – Head Position

The two most usual pieces of advice given to women golfers are 'keep your head down' and 'watch the ball'. You need to understand just what both these pieces of advice mean during play.

You need to look at the back of the ball – the part you are trying to hit. By the top of the backswing your head should turn very slightly and your left eye should now see the ball. The view from the right eye is probably hidden by your nose. Watch the ball but allow your head a little freedom.

In the correct position (see opposite page) your left shoulder covers your chin, your head turns slightly in the backswing and all you should see is the ball and first tee peg shown in the photograph. You should not see your feet. Through impact you should certainly watch the ball as you hit it and your head should be able to stay still well after the ball has gone.

Another example of the perfect position is shown in the picture of top American golfer Emilee Klein, on page 57.

WRONG
If you stare at the ball too intently your head dips down over your left shoulder, as in the photograph to the right. The problem can also be caused by playing the ball too far left in the stance as a beginner.

WRONG
If you stare at the ball and keep your head too still, again this is the likely position (see right). Yes you can see the ball, and you can probably also see your feet

If you find yourself constantly coming up through impact you may get the wrong relationship between right shoulder and chin. This is a fault women commonly have. In this fault the right shoulder is under the chin through impact and literally forces the head up beyond impact. If you are long in the neck and narrow across the shoulders, it is even more likely to happen.

TRY THIS EXERCISE
Practise getting the right relationship of shoulders and chin – your left shoulder should cover the chin in the backswing and the right one cover it in the throughswing. Practise swinging back and through to feel the relationship of chin and shoulders – and do it with your mouth open. This gives an even more definite feeling of chin and shoulder. Remember that this is a woman's problem! Men just don't do it.

REMEMBER
CHIN IN

The Sway – Hips not Head

A woman's physique is obviously different from that of a man.
Women are more supple in the joints, smaller in the shoulders and
larger in the hips. This causes certain swing problems that men
rarely encounter. Here is one of them.

WRONG

A common swing fault amongst women is
generally known as a sway. If told that you
sway, it won't be your head that is swaying
from side to side but your hips. Even so, your
instinct will be to try to keep your head still.
However, you need to give your head a little
more freedom.

WRONG

This kind of posture will often cause a sway.
With the bottom in instead of out at address,
the hips naturally move from side to side.
The first step to correcting a sway is to
produce good posture at address. Stick
your bottom out and up and keep it well
out during your backswing.

To correct the sway, don't be afraid of exaggerating the change. It is gained by bending over at address from the hips, staying bending over with the bottom out and allowing the top half to turn. Your head must feel as though it moves several inches behind the ball. Keep the ball central in the stance and allow your top half to turn, left eye looking at the ball. Think of right ear down to give your head the freedom it needs.

To practise the feeling, bend over without a club in your hand and turn your body. Now stand a little more upright, then a little more upright again – until you adopt your golfing posture. In the backswing the posture should stay constant, keeping your backside towards the target, turning your shoulders and allowing your head to move just enough.

ANOTHER EXERCISE
Set up with a tennis ball held by your right groin and make the feeling of a backswing. In the correct backswing, the tennis ball will stay there. The wrong backswing with the hip sway will release the ball.

REMEMBER
BOTTOM OUT – KEEP IT OUT!

Going for Distance

Every golfer wants to hit the ball further. Even the longest of hitters – such as Laura Davies – would like more length! Physical strength obviously plays its part, but so does good timing.

PERFECT FOLLOWTHROUGH
Don't be afraid to loosen up enough to achieve your own perfect followthrough. This is the essential ingredient of achieving greater distance in your shots.

REMEMBER: Make the loudest contact you can.

The first key to good distance is being loose enough and free enough to find a perfect followthrough. If you don't know where the club will land at the end of the swing, your body naturally resists creating maximum clubhead speed.

The wrist action through impact is like throwing a ball. When urged to find more distance, most women say they feel out of control. You have to feel sufficiently out of control to allow the speed to happen. If you aren't good at throwing a ball, think of shaking the mercury down a clinical thermometer. Your fingers hold the thermometer firmly enough so that you don't drop it. The wrist has to be loose enough to flick and make speed. It is that same sort of suddenness to the wrists which creates speed in the golfswing.

The key to getting good distance is perfect timing. Don't rush the swing in trying to hit hard. You need to time it. The fastest part of the swing needs to be at impact and not before or after. Stand on the driving range and try to make the loudest noise you can on the back of the ball. The louder the noise the further the ball travels.

If you want a really long drive on the golf course then don't press for distance. Just focus on the back of the ball and listen for the loudest sound you can make on contact. That preserves your tempo and rhythm.

Checkpoints

Alison Nicholas, at just 1.52m (5ft) tall is an outstandingly long hitter just through technique and timing.

For club woman golfers the key to getting maximum distance is the hand and wrist action through impact. The hands and fingers should grip firmly but the wrists must be loose enough to generate speed. As an exercise, practise swinging back and through, back and through repeatedly with a 5, 6, or 7 iron. The forearms need to turn, allowing the wrists to cross over and speed to be generated.

Remember that loose = long. The looser you are the more clubhead speed you are likely to generate and the further the ball will travel. If by contrast you are stiff, the shots are short. This wrist action requires the left arm to fold away correctly in the throughswing. At address the left elbow should point slightly downward and is then allowed to fold away as you swing through. Don't allow thoughts of a straight left arm to make that left arm too stiff beyond impact.

To strengthen your wrists, practise swinging with a weighted club. You can buy special golfing weights to fit down at the neck of the clubhead.

Alternatively, practise swishing the club in thick grass to strengthen your hands and improve your control.

ALISON NICHOLAS
Although she is not very tall, Alison Nicholas of England is one of the longest hitters in the women's game.

REMEMBER
LOOSE = LONG

Going for Direction

Women golfers have far fewer problems with the direction of shots than do most men. The further you hit the ball, of course, the more important direction becomes.

If you have directional problems, it is important to understand the mechanics of the club and the ball. Without this, learning is mere superstition. You should appreciate that a golf ball is designed to take up spin. The dimples on the surface encourage spin, which helps to get the ball airborne. In taking up backspin, the ball also takes up sidespin with great ease.

In most ball games, the ball flies straight and you have to learn to put spin on the ball to make it curve. In golf, you first have to learn to take sidespin off the ball to get it flying straight. Then the good player learns to put spin back on to bend the ball as required. This may be done either to curve shots round obstacles, for a different spin, or to hold them into a wind.

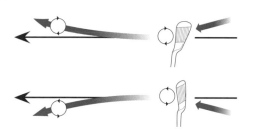

DIRECTIONAL DIFFICULTIES

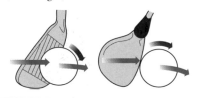

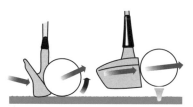

RULES TO REMEMBER

1 The more lofted the club, the greater the backspin and the less sidespin will take effect. It is difficult, for example, to bend a ball with a 9 iron. In contrast, the driver produces very little backspin and easily takes up sidespin. Any hook or slice is exaggerated. It is far easier to hit a 5 wood straight than to hit a driver straight.

2 Provided the ball is struck from the middle or near middle of the clubface, it starts in the direction of the swing.

3 A correctly struck ball starting left is produced by a left-aimed swing – 'out-to-in'. It may then bend left or right, depending on the clubface angle.

4 Analyse any shot in terms of 'Where did it start? How did it curve?' and you will begin to get a clue to any fault in your swing.

The loft of an iron naturally gets the clubface beneath the back of the ball (above left) and produces backspin. The loft of a driver (above right) produces much less backspin and a longer, lower shot.

Lofted clubs hit the ball at the bottom producing backspin but very little sidespin (below left). The driver hits the ball near its equator, producing lots of sidespin if the clubface is open or closed (below right).

THE FADE
The ball starts on target, drifting away slightly to the right with a curve. Professionals often like to hit their iron shots like this. The ball lands and stops well.

THE PUSH FADE
An in-to-out attack starts the ball right of target. An open clubface sees it bend further right. The followthrough is probably incomplete, with a weak grip or stiff wrists.

THE SLICE
An out-to-in swing starts the ball left and also imparts cutspin to the shot. Think of this as being like a cut shot with a tennis racquet, stiff wrists and an up and down action.

THE PUSH
An in-to-out attack with the clubface square. The ball flies straight right. Women invariably do this through aiming off to the right.

THE DRAW
The clubface is fractionally closed in relation to the direction of the swing. The ball bends very slightly from right to left and kicks and runs on landing. Many think this is the perfect shot.

THE PULL HOOK
The ball starting left from an out-to-in swing with a closed clubface bending it even further. Usually comes from a poor grip, right hand underneath. It is like exaggerated topspin with a tennis racquet.

THE HOOK
The shot starting to the right of your stance with the clubface closed through impact. Look for the ball being too far back in your stance, right hand wrongly underneath like a tennis player.

THE PULL
An out-to-in attack, starting the ball left with the clubface square. Caused by aiming to the right and dragging to the left.

REMEMBER
CHECK YOUR AIMING!

84 Curing the Push and Pull

The push is a shot which flies straight out to the right of the target and a pull is one which flies straight left of the target. If you aim correctly it is comparatively difficult to push a ball to the right but extremely easy to turn your body and pull it to the left.

GETTING IT RIGHT
The point of impact is the most important part of every swing you make, because it is this that has the greatest influence on the direction of shot. If you push the ball, it will fly straight right. If you pull it, it will go left. Here Liselotte Neumann of Sweden shows how it should be done.

If you push the ball straight to the right or pull it to the left, check your aiming. More women golfers tend to aim off to the right than aim straight – indeed, it is probably the most common fault in the women's game. If you aim to the right, you may hit odd shots to the right. Alternatively you may find yourself turning your body and dragging the ball away to the left.

The cure to this problem is to practise aiming over a spot. If you either pull or push the shot, hold your followthrough, then return your right foot back to its starting point. Place your club on the ground in front of your shoes. Walk round behind the ball and check your aiming. The line of your toes should be parallel to your shot.

If you push the ball to the right, check your ball position. If the ball is behind centre in the stance your clubhead strikes it with a swing still travelling out to the right. The same can happen if you sway to the left through impact.

If you push the ball to the right, perhaps with a little bend at the end of the flight, you will probably find your hips facing to the right at the end of the swing. Correct this by ensuring that your left leg turns out of the

THE PUSH SHOT FAULT
If you set the ball too far back in your stance, or line up wrongly aiming to the right, you will invariably push the ball out to the right.

THE PULL SHOT FAULT
Trying to compensate for aiming too far right will often mean that you drag your shoulders across the shot and pull the ball to the left.

way and that your hips really do face the target in your followthrough.

If you pull the ball to the left you instinctively start aiming to the right. The further right you aim the more you tend to drag the ball round with your shoulders and pull it to the left. Make sure that you finish with a high followthrough and the clubshaft coming directly over your shoulders. If you pull the ball left, you will find your shoulders facing way left at the end of the followthrough. Feel that the followthrough is on your target.

It is easy to hit to the left – an 'out-to-in' swing. It is difficult to hit from the inside with the correct curved path. To produce the correct 'inside' attack, the clubhead should feel as though it comes from behind you. Like swinging a tennis racquet, you swing it in a curve.

Practise the exercise hitting through the ball like a hammer and nail (pp. 50–1). Try to feel a shallow attack, attacking the ball from behind your legs. If you pull the ball to the left, the chances are you also play it too far forward in your stance. Play the ball back towards the middle of the stance and try for a shallow, inside attack.

REMEMBER
WORK ON YOUR AIMING

Curing a Hook

A hook shot starts off in the same way as a push but bends sharply back to the left. Its main cause is a closed clubface at impact.

1 To feel the correct grip make sure your right hand is really facing the target and not up toward your face. Adjust your left hand if necessary. Don't grip the club like a tennis racquet, as though trying to hit the ball up into the air. Keep your hand facing forward.

Check the position of your right thumb and index finger. If your right thumb is too loosely round to the side of the club it can allow the wrists to move too freely. Bring the right thumb a little closer down the front of the club for firmer wrists.

WHAT CAN BE WRONG?

If the right hand is too much underneath at address it will tend to turn the club over through impact, closing it and hooking the ball.

If you shut the clubface in the takeaway, face down instead of toe up, you are already on the way to hooking.

If you take the club away face down you produce a shut face at the top of the backswing and it remains shut in the followthrough.

If your grip is perfect, you may simply have a tennis player's instinct of making an action like a topspin forehand, rolling the face over.

2 The clubface should correctly move from toe up in the backswing to toe up in the throughswing and not face down. You may need to feel as though you hold the clubface up slightly beyond impact.

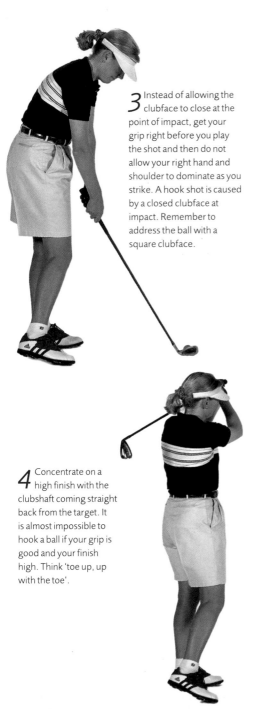

3 Instead of allowing the clubface to close at the point of impact, get your grip right before you play the shot and then do not allow your right hand and shoulder to dominate as you strike. A hook shot is caused by a closed clubface at impact. Remember to address the ball with a square clubface.

4 Concentrate on a high finish with the clubshaft coming straight back from the target. It is almost impossible to hook a ball if your grip is good and your finish high. Think 'toe up, up with the toe'.

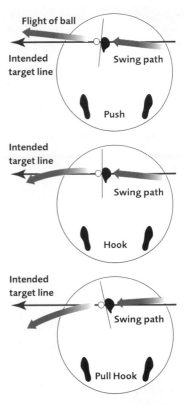

Flight of ball
Intended target line
Swing path
Push

Intended target line
Swing path
Hook

Intended target line
Swing path
Pull Hook

WHAT CAUSES PUSHES, PULLS AND HOOKS?

A push (top) is caused by an in-to-out swing, with the clubface square to the swing path. A hook (centre) is caused by an in-to-out swing from a square stance, with the clubface more or less square to the target. Do not confuse a pull hook with a hook. In a pull hook (above), players often have an out-to-in swing and a poor grip which closes the clubface. They then aim off to the right to counteract this.

REMEMBER DON'T LET THE RIGHT HAND UNDER

The slice shot is a weak – and very common – shot that curves to the right and spins to right on landing. It tends not to go as far as intended and is rather like a cut shot with a tennis racquet.

A slice usually comes from stiffness in the wrists. Remember that stiff = short = slice. Loose=long=left. As the first point of correction, loosen up and relax.

A slice is often caused by a weak grip, with the left hand too far round to the right. You may also wrongly put your right thumb straight down the front. Check that you see most of the logo on the back of your glove. Keep the right thumb well round to the left on the grip. This will feel looser and may feel out of control but it allows the clubface to work properly.

You need to feel the clubface face down beyond impact. Think of it facing down to the grass and not up to the sky as you move on through. Changing your grip will help this happen. Experiment with putting your left hand further over and your right further under until you can bend the ball to the left. But work at the clubface.

Remember that the left arm stays straight in the backswing but mustn't be stiff. Beyond impact it must fold out of the way to allow the wrists and clubface to turn. Practise holding the club in your left hand and putting your right hand just above your left elbow. Swing back and through, allowing the left arm to fold.

If you are a good racquet player, cure a tendency to slice golf shots by thinking of playing topspin rather than cutspin.

If you slice the ball, particularly with a driver, feel that your arms stay close together

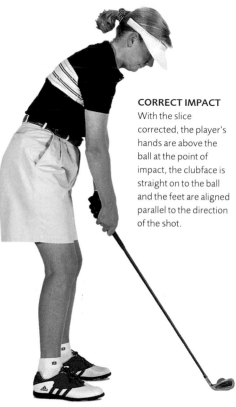

CORRECT IMPACT
With the slice corrected, the player's hands are above the ball at the point of impact, the clubface is straight on to the ball and the feet are aligned parallel to the direction of the shot.

in the throughswing. Allow the right arm to climb over the left, feel the left arm in and under, and the clubface turning over.

WRONG
If you slice the ball away to the right your clubface comes through face up. Your left arm may be too stiff or you may simply have the wrong concept of how the clubface should work.

SLICE IMPACT

At the moment of impact in a sliced shot, typically the golfer's hands are too far ahead of the ball through impact and the clubface is wide open, forcing the ball out to the right.

SLICE IMPACT (2)

This is what the slicer's action looks like from the side. Slicers tend to aim their feet left to counteract their problem and then only make things worse by swinging across the ball to the left.

Swing path out-to-in

Target path

Swing path in-to-out

Open face

DIRECTION OF THE SLICE

With her hands too far ahead of the ball at impact and the clubface wide open, the slicer hits out-to-in or in-to-out, causing her slice, instead of along the straight target path.

THE SLICER'S FEET

Instead of lining their feet up correctly, parallel to the line of the shot (the black lines in the diagram), slicers tend to compensate for their problem by lining their feet up to the left (blue lines) and making the slice worse by hitting across the ball.

REMEMBER
LOOSEN UP

Slicing – the Out-to-In Swing

Most golfers who slice the ball away to the right with an open clubface start swinging up and down in an out-to-in direction. You instinctively try to keep the ball to the left. The swing then cuts across the ball and usually exaggerates the slice and makes it worse.

The first correction should always be to stop the clubface staying open. Sort out your grip, loosen up and allow the clubface to turn.

Once the grip is corrected, the slice usually changes into shots pulled straight left and swing corrections become easier.

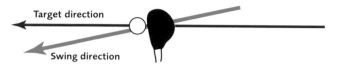

CLOSE THE CLUBFACE
An open clubface is the single biggest cause of a sliced shot. Check your grip and get the clubface closed – but not *too* closed!

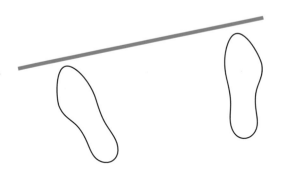

SWINGING OUT-TO-IN
By lining up aiming left – in attempting to counteract the slice – slicers actually exacerbate their problem by producing an out-to-in swing across the line of the shot, and adding sidespin.

1 Slicers usually try to keep the ball left with their body and shoulders, producing an out-to-in swing. This produces a steep attack with more downward power and less forward power.

2 Once you have sorted out the clubface, learn to hit the ball from the inside. Feel that you make a more rounded backswing and a curved path through impact. Again think of the way you swing a tennis racquet from round behind yourself and not up and down. Feel that you attack the ball from behind your legs.

3 The right side of the body, particularly the right hip or right shoulder, can easily become dominant. From the top of the backswing think of hitting along the line of your hips.

4 On a driving range, practise with a drinks can or clubhead cover positioned about 37.5cm (15in) directly behind the ball. Stand parallel to your target and miss the obstacle on the backswing and when you attack the ball.

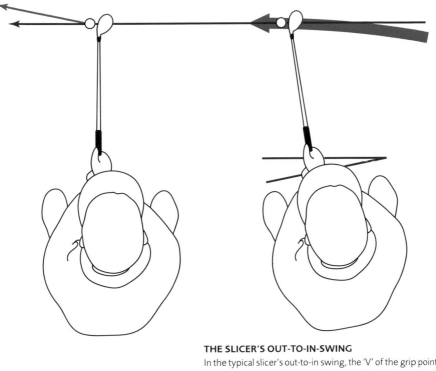

THE SLICER'S OUT-TO-IN-SWING

In the typical slicer's out-to-in swing, the 'V' of the grip points incorrectly to the chin and not the right shoulder, as it should do; the clubface is open, the feet aim left and the shoulders move across the line of the shot at the point of impact. The effect is like cutspin with a tennis racquet.

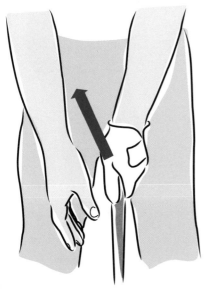

CHECK THE GRIP

The grip is very important. Any tendency for the Vs to point to the chin will produce an open clubface. Keep the left hand well on top, the right under the club, with the Vs to the right shoulder. The interlocking grip can be too tight. Try the Vardon or baseball grip instead and look for looseness in the hands and wrists.

REMEMBER
THINK OF TOPSPIN WITH A RACQUET

Doing *Your* Best Swing More Often

If you can make your best swing 95 percent of the time instead of 50 percent of the time, you will play better golf. The key is found in improving your followthrough and balance.

To improve your golf the first stage is not necessarily to change your swing, but to learn to do your best swing more often. Most club golfers produce a variety of swings, particularly with too much variation in the followthrough. Here are four tips.

ADDRESS

BALANCE

YOUR BEST SWING
Remember that good golf is all about learning to make your best swing more often. For good players, improvement is often a question of making your bad shots better and less destructive.

Address. This position is a rehearsal of impact. Make your address position feel comfortable, then practise swinging to the top of your backswing. Just as important, practise swinging through to your followthrough. This way you get good posture, stand tall, and learn to rehearse your contact.

Think B for balance. And B for breathing, rather than B for backswing. Learn to hold the followthrough and be able to count 'one, two, three, four'. Make every followthrough identical.

Contact. Work at the sound of your contact and see the grass after the ball has gone! If your contact isn't good, guard against having the ball too far left in your stance – keep it just ahead of centre. Remember, the louder the noise on the ball, the better and further the ball flies. Practise improving your contact sound at a driving range.

Discipline. Create a real and deliberate routine for addressing the ball. Remember that more women golfers tend to aim off to the right than aim straight.

CONTACT   DISCIPLINE

REMEMBER
MAKE YOUR
BAD SHOTS
BETTER!

The Power of Putting

For a scratch golfer or professional, almost 50 percent of any shots in a round are played with a putter. For high handicappers, putting usually accounts for 40 percent of the score. For every player, the putter is possibly the most important club in the golf bag. In this chapter we look at choosing a putter and using it in different situations.

You will find a wide range of putters on sale and you should spend time finding a good one as you will be using it a lot. If you are under 1.72 metres (5ft 8in) tall, you need a ladies' length putter, which is 82.5cm (33in) long. The standard men's length is 87.5cm (35in) and is designed for a player of 1.83 metres (6ft) or more tall.

How to choose your putter

Putters come in various styles: blade, mallet, centre-shafted and heel-toe. You should look for one with heel-toe weighting which gives a large 'sweetspot' for an accurate hit. To check the sweetspot, hang the putter between thumb and index finger. With a coin or your fingernail, tap from the toe toward the heel. The sweetspot is the area where you feel no twisting. The larger it is, the easier the putter will be to use.

The putter should have a line marked in the centre of the top of the head which you use to aim at the hole. It is easier to aim the line at the hole than to aim the face at the hole.

Check the putter's balance – see that it is face-balanced rather than toe-heavy. If perfectly balanced, the face should sit horizontally, if you balance it from the shaft.

The grip on the shaft should be flat-fronted and curved to encourage your grip and wrist position.

A putter must always have a lie of at least 10 degrees between the shaft and the vertical. The more upright your putter sits, the easier you will find it to use.

A putter always has a little loft – between 3 and 5 degrees. If you play on a course with very slow greens, a more lofted putter is suitable.

Catrin Nilsmark of Sweden measures up a putt at the Evian Masters tournament in France.

The Putting Grip

You should use a completely different grip for the putter. With the long shots you want looseness and freedom in the wrists for distance. With putting you want firm wrists. The grip is also used for other short shots.

The long game grip (below left) must allow the clubhead to turn beyond impact. The good putting grip holds the clubface up beyond impact.

The putting grip used by nearly all professional golfers is the reverse overlap grip (below right). It aims to keep the wrists firm and the clubface working correctly.

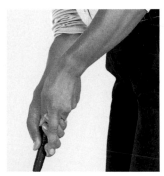

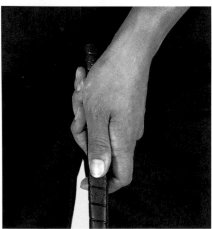

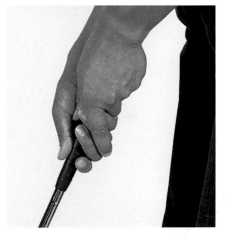

1 The left hand is positioned well to the left on the club. You should not be able to see your knuckles or the logo on your glove. The thumb is straight down the front of the grip. The clubshaft runs up through the fold in your hand, very different from your long game grip.

2 To add the right hand, hang the left index finger out. Put the heel of the right hand against the other three fingers of the left hand and complete the grip with the pad of your right thumb on the front of the grip. The left index finger sits on the outside. The most common position is to sit it on the third finger of the right hand.

3 In a perfect putting grip the right hand is pulled up high on the left hand so that the second and third finger of the left hand are inside the palm of the right hand. This keeps the two hands united – and is much better than having the right hand totally below the left hand.

4 Both thumbs should be visible. The left hand should be turned well round to the left, with the left thumb showing, not hidden as it is in the long game grip. The putting grip is much more open.

To create the right position, hold the club out in front of you and arch the wrists. If you can't achieve this position, both hands are probably too much on the top of the club. Allow them both to be turned slightly beneath it. You should see both thumbs but not your knuckles

5 For short putting you may like to put the right index finger down the back of the grip. It is traditionally known as the 'after forty finger grip', the idea being that it steadies the grip for slightly older players, who presumably might have shakier hands than their younger counterparts!

EXPERT TIP
If you do put the right index finger down the back of the grip to steady the putter, be sure not to wrap it too far under the shaft so that the finger starts to pull the putter off-line as you make the stroke.

REMEMBER
LEFT INDEX FINGER OUT

The Putting Stance

Most club golfers make the mistake of not having putting lessons, often on the assumption that you can either putt naturally or you can't at all. But there is plenty to learn about putting.

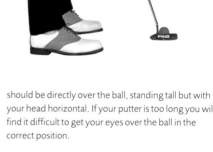

1 Sit the putter flat on its bottom without tipping your hands forward. The ball should be positioned just ahead of centre in your stance and directly under your eyes. Use a comfortable width of stance with your feet roughly the width of your hips. The elbows should feel slightly turned backwards and into your body, the inside of your arms facing forward.

2 The correct length of putter is crucial for a good address position (see p. 94). Your feet should be parallel to the line of your putt, the club sitting flat on its bottom, your wrists slightly arched. Your eyes

should be directly over the ball, standing tall but with your head horizontal. If your putter is too long you will find it difficult to get your eyes over the ball in the correct position.

3 The putter head should sit flat on its bottom. This helps to keep the club travelling back and through with a straight stroke (above). Make sure you position the ball in the middle of the clubface at address. You will see later (pp. 104–5) how to adjust this for sidehill putts. But for a straight putt, address the ball in the middle of the clubface and hit it from the middle of the clubface.

4 When you address the ball there should always be a little gap – say 1cm (½in) – between the putter head and the ball so there is no danger of wobbling it. Hold the club very slightly off the ground – it should feel as though it *hangs* from your arms and shoulders, so that you are very definitely supporting its weight before you make your swing. A putter should always swing just above the ground, never brushing the grass (see diagram right).

Never hold the club too loosely. Always hold it firmly enough so that you are in control of the putter at address. Certainly never lean on it.

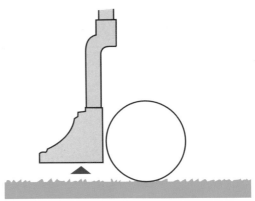

5 Use a putter with a line on. Check that the line corresponds with the sweetspot of the putter and position the ball directly opposite.

WRONG
If your putter is too long or your wrists sit too low, the toe of the club will wrongly be off the ground. This encourages an incorrect curved stroke.

REMEMBER
HANG THE
PUTTER

Many golfers find it difficult to aim a putter correctly. Even professionals have problems and constantly ask a caddie to check their address position before they play their putt.

AIMING YOUR PUTTER
A putter with a line on is usually easier to aim than a putter without one. Aim the line rather than aiming the face. At address, stand over the ball with your head horizontal and the line on the putter straight at the centre of the back of the ball.

Even with a 1 metre (3ft) putt many golfers find it difficult to aim straight. The more common error is to aim away to the right. If you miss short putts to the right check your aiming. Some professionals meticulously line up the writing on the ball to aim at the hole – but that can be time-consuming!

Try this exercise. On a carpet or flat green set up three points in a line. Look from behind your ball. Put a small coin 45cm (18in) ahead of it and a tee peg 1.83 metres (6ft) away to aim to. Address your ball. At address, if you aim correctly, the coin should appear on line to the tee peg. If the coin looks to be too far left, then your tendency is to aim away to the right – the more common error. If the coin appears to move to the right then your tendency is to aim to the left. Try adjusting your head position to see if all three line up.

If your tendency is to aim away to the right, don't just line up over a spot in front of you. Try to choose a little spot fractionally right of the line of your putt and feel as though you line up to aim just left of it.

Your head position can be important for lining up. In theory, if your eyes are too far over the ball you are more likely to aim left.

CHECK YOUR AIMING
When you have lined up your putt, let go of the club with your right hand, still holding it with your left, and squat down behind it to check the putter is aiming straight.

PRACTISE SHORT PUTTING
Set up balls from 45cm (18in) to 2.4m (8ft) from the hole. Start with the closest and work through the line. If you miss one, start again.

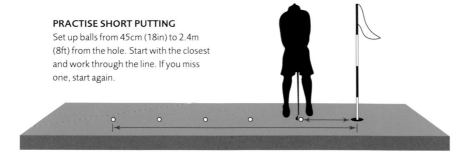

If your eyes are inside the ball then you are more likely to aim off to the right. But experiment with your head position until you learn to see a straight line.

Check your aiming. Adopt your address position, let go with your right hand, keep hold of the club with your left hand and go round behind it to see if the putter is aiming straight. Some women professionals aim the putter from behind the ball in this way then walk round to take up their address position. But if you adopt this method, learn to do it quickly!

At address your head should be horizontal, not up, as in the long game. When you line up putts, your head should swivel to see the line rather than lifting and turning.

Our ability to aim can vary with lengths of putt. With a very short putt both eyes see the ball and hole. With a slightly longer putt your left eye sees the ball and the hole but the view from your right eye is hidden by your nose. With a longer putt still you can't see the ball and hole at the same time. Check your aiming at each length.

REMEMBER
USE A PUTTER
WITH A
LINE ON

The Short Putting Stroke

Short putting requires good aiming and a good stroke.
Find a perfectly flat putt on which to practise – just a
putt the length of your putter.

A good putting stroke should always be back
and through and stop. Remember to hang
the putter slightly off the ground so that you
are in control of it at address. This allows you
to make a slow, not jerky, stroke. Swing the
putter back a few inches – don't be too fussy
about the length – and then through into a
stationary finish. The stroke should be from
the arms and shoulders, with the left wrist
staying firm. At the end of a good stroke the
head and eyes should remain still, left wrist
firm, putter face upward.

The most common faulty stroke is for the
clubface to turn left through impact.

At the end of the stroke your head should
be down and your eyes focused on the grass
where the ball was. Remember, it isn't
possible to lose a ball with a short putt! In
fact, most people very rarely lose a ball with
any length putt!

You should see the ball out of the corner
of your left eye or simply hear it drop in the
hole. As an exercise, practise with a coin
behind the ball. Hang the club slightly off

the ground, look at the coin and stay looking at the coin as the ball goes in the hole. This will train you to keep your head still and make you realize that you see it out the corner of your left eye. This is only an exercise and you mustn't leave the coin or ball marker there on the green.

A good putting stroke is a combination of arms and shoulders with no wrist action. The head should stay still but the shoulders must move. As an exercise, lay another club down on the ground. Position your ball just opposite the end of the club. This allows you to swing the clubhead slightly inside on the backswing. Whether inside or straight back doesn't matter – just remember never outside. The key then is to keep your clubhead travelling through and up the line of the other club, never crossing it. To make a good stroke think: 'Left shoulder up, ball in the cup.' Not: 'Right shoulder round, still above ground!'

Keep the head and eyes still, back through and stop in a face up position for perfect short putting.

PERFECT SHORT PUTTING
Keep your head perfectly still and feel the putter hanging from your arms and shoulders before you make the stroke. Always swing the putter above the ground (opposite).

ADDRESS
This is what your putting address should look like from side on.

FEEL THE PUTTER
For short putts, be sure to *feel* the putter moving in a straight path.

HEAD STILL
Keep your head still and your eyes looking at the spot where the ball was after it has left the putter.

REMEMBER
KEEP YOUR HEAD AND EYES STILL

Making Good Sidehill Putts

Unfortunately not all the putts we get on the course are completely straight. But the key to good sidehill putting is to remember that every putt should be treated as a straight putt.

To be a good short putter, keep practising putts of 1 metre (3ft). From 1 metre we should get a 100 percent record. You start learning about your own putting. Practising with a straight putt develops a good stroke. However, unfortunately it is very easy on a sidehill lie to lose your best stroke.

On a sidehill lie with the ball slightly above your feet the tendency is to lose your straight stroke and to allow the putt to become a curve. Choose a spot to the right of the hole where you know you have to aim. Remember that your feet are slightly below the ball, so try to stand a little taller to counteract this. Having chosen the spot you are aiming for, make a perfectly straight stroke to that spot and try to ignore the hole.

CHECK Don't allow your stroke to become a curve, as though following the slope and trying to steer the ball around the curve.

In playing a right to left putt, address the ball much nearer the toe of the club. This helps to keep the ball travelling slowly and also helps to keep the ball spinning up slightly to the right. As long as the ball is above the hole, it will always have a chance of dropping down and into it.

The speed of the sidehill putt is much more crucial than with a straight putt. It is a combination of line and length. If you over-hit, the ball turns down to the hole too late. If you under-hit, it turns too early. The speed of the putt always has to be carefully judged.

On a sidehill putt some professionals like to hit the ball very hard straight for the back of the hole. This counteracts the borrow, but if you do miss, the ball will go alarmingly far past. If you prefer to hit the putt more softly, you have to allow much more to the right. But do remember to practise on the practice green with the same speed you would use on the course. Many players hit the ball firmly and straight on the practice green but then lack the courage to do this on the course!

On a left to right putt, try the following approach. Choose a spot to the left of the hole. Bend at the knees very slightly to counteract the slope, sit the club slightly on its heel with the toe fractionally off the ground and address the ball in the neck of the club. Addressing the ball towards the heel helps keep the ball slightly to the left and stops it sliding away to the right. It does mean that the ball travels off a little more quickly, so treat it with caution!

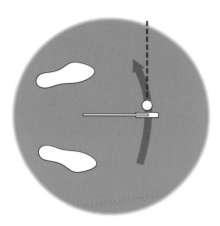

DON'T CURVE THE PUTT

Don't be tempted with a right-to-left putt, for example, to move your putter in a curved path (above). Always play straight back and through.

PLAY A STRAIGHT PUTT

Whatever point you choose to aim for, always play a straight putt (above).

AIM DEFINITELY

Whether you choose a straight, firm putt or a softer one to allow for the slope, always aim and play straight to a definite aiming point.

REMEMBER
KEEP A
STRAIGHT
STROKE

Short Putting Practice

Practice is vital to success in any area of golf and none the less so in putting. After all, remember that putting can make up as much as 40 percent of your game as a high handicapper and even more as you improve at your handicap.

To become a good short putter, practise repeatedly from 1 metre (3ft). From this distance you really should be able to get a 100 percent success rate. Firstly, this gives you confidence. Secondly, if you miss putts you get feedback. You start learning about your own stroke. Even putting machines cannot get the ball in the hole every time from 1.5 metres (5ft) or 1.83 metres (6ft), so

putting from these distances you lose confidence and learn far less. If you learn to become a good putter from 1 metre (3ft), you soon get more confidence with your long putting and your chipping from around the green. So, practise from 1 metre with a straight putt and see how many you can get in. Set a target, whether 20, 50, or 100, and don't go home until you achieve it!

Line up a row of six balls from 0.6 metre – 2.4 metres (2–8ft). Try to keep your head and eyes still and keep your same good short putting stroke as you progress further along the line. If you should miss one, take the balls out and start all over again. By the time you get to the last putt, your head and eyes should stay still and you should hear the ball drop in!

WRONG
Don't practise by going from one ball to the next (left). The danger is that you aim the first ball correctly and then aim the second and third ones away to the right.

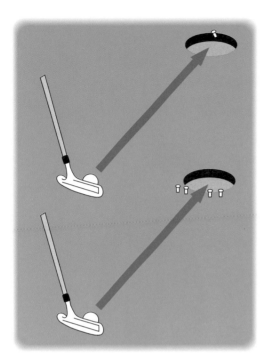

Narrow the hole with two tee pegs placed either side. Practise like this and the hole, without restrictions, should seem like a bucket!

To encourage a good followthrough, practise from just 35–45cm (14–18in) with a push stroke. Don't make a backswing. Just roll the ball through and feel your clubhead go toward your target with the clubface upward. This is an illegal stroke, so do it just as an exercise, from a maximum of 45 cm (18in) and never just before playing.

Practise with a coin behind the ball. This encourages you to hang the putter from your arms and shoulders. Stay looking at the marker to keep your head and eyes still.

Put a tee peg in the back of the hole. Learn to make the ball hit the tee peg as it drops in. This teaches you to be positive rather than under-hitting putts. A putt travelling too slowly can wobble off line before it reaches the hole. A firmly hit putt holds its line.

Some players do well on the practice green and not on the course. Make your normal practice to keep repeating the same straight putt. But to practise for the pressure of the golf course, put four balls round the hole in a circle. Treat each putt as if it were to win a tournament. Mark it with a marker, turn the ball round so that the writing faces the hole or lines up with the hole – just as you prefer. Do a practice swing or don't do a practice swing. It's up to you.

Use exactly the technique you intend to use on the course. Make each putt count. Take the same time and care you do on the course. Marking the ball is all part of the routine.

As a winter exercise, try putting with a weighted cotton reel on a fast running surface. If you don't meet the cotton reel squarely, it won't run truly!

REMEMBER
PRACTISE
FROM 1 METRE
(3FT)

Long Putting

Good long putting is all about judging distance rather than judging direction. Remember that if you three-putt it will nearly always be because you hit the ball the wrong distance and not because you have hit it crooked.

Before every long putt, always have one or two practice swings to try to feel the distance. The length of your practice swing should rehearse your intentions with the ball. The longer the putt the longer the swing. The swing should be made predominantly with the arms and shoulders – not just the shoulders – but with reasonably firm wrists.

One of the worst things you can do with the ball is to brush the ground. The ball won't run truly. So make sure your practice swing is as close to the ground as possible without touching it. Most players tend to underswing on a long putt. The feeling should be of a long, smooth, stroke without any added hit

at the bottom of the swing. Think of the timing of a long, slow brush stroke.

It is important to make a good strike on the back of the ball. Remember that you are very unlikely to lose a ball with a putt. The occasional 'pro' has been seen to putt off the green into a water hazard, but it is very unusual. Learn to look at the ball as you hit it. Practise holding the finish of the stroke and counting 'one, two, three', before you look up. You soon become aware of seeing the ball out of the corner of your left eye. Staying down will encourage you to get a good strike on it. You can often feel the quality of your putt simply through the contact. Different

PRACTICE STROKES
You need to 'feel' the distance with long putting strokes, so be sure to take a couple of smooth practice swings before you address the actual putt (opposite).

PRACTISING LONG PUTTS
To concentrate on length rather than direction, putt the ball back to the edge of the green after completing each hole (above). However, it is probably best only to do this when the course is empty! Be sure not to hold up others' play.

CHOOSING YOUR LINE
Choose a definite spot to aim to, but remember that for good putting judging distance is the key.

golf balls respond differently. On a perfectly flat green of reasonable speed, a soft-covered ball can travel one metre shorter than a harder ball on a 10 metre (11 yard) putt. Get used to one make of ball. They do respond differently.

Don't try to hole a long putt. Simply concentrate on getting it as close as possible. In this way you are more likely to think about the distance than the direction. If you become obsessed with the line of the putt, it is easy to forget the distance. Unfortunately most men judge distance better than most women. That is why they become better racing drivers – particularly in the club car park!

On a sidehill putt, assess whether you have to hit the ball slightly to the right or slightly to the left. Remember that with someone attending the flag you can always ask them to stand whichever side of the hole you prefer. You may find it easier to feel you are aiming slightly towards their feet than to the hole itself. But once you are allowing to the side, still concentrate more on your distance than on the line. Just concentrate on hitting a straight putt to the point you have chosen but focus more than anything on the length of your stroke and rolling the ball at the right speed.

REMEMBER
DISTANCE IS HARDER THAN DIRECTION

Reading Greens

Greens aren't always flat and you need to understand the
slope. You need to judge not only whether you need to
borrow to the left or borrow to the right on a side slope but
also whether you are putting uphill or downhill.

In order to read the green, look for the
overall slope. Look for the overall lie of
the land. If you have walked downhill
to the green the green is probably also
downhill. If the whole fairway slopes
from one side to the other, then the
green probably follows the same angle.
When you are playing on a course you
don't know, try to get to the green
slightly before your playing partners
and have time to walk quickly round to
the back of it to get the feeling of the
overall slope. The odds are that your
putt will follow the overall slope and
lie of the land.

ASSESS THE GREEN
Look at the hole to
check the grain of
the grass and any
imperfections just
near the hole.

The world is round, but when we
look at the small section within our
vision it looks reasonably flat. Much
the same applies to the green. If you bend
down and start looking at too small a section,
you can confuse yourself. Most players read a
green better by taking an overall view of it
than by looking at too small an area.
Certainly the part nearest the hole is the most
important. The ball is slowing up then and
will take up more break. But always keep the
overall slope of the green in mind.

It is usually easy to see if you are going
uphill, but it can be difficult to see a
downslope. Many players hit the ball too
hard and will then say 'I didn't realize I was
going downhill'. If you walk onto a green
that appears dead flat, take care. It may be
downhill – particularly if the fairway
approaching it was downhill.

Modern courses are usually built with the
back of the green higher than the front of

the green. On this 'normal' green, all putts
from the front are uphill, putts from the back
downhill. Those putts taken from the right
of the green are always right to left and putts
from the left of the green are left to right.
With this piece of information in mind you
can usually read a sidehill putt quite simply.
The difficult putts are those from above the
hole. 'Am I on the right to left section? Have I
crossed the line and am I on the left to right
section?' The most difficult putt is the one
almost directly above the hole. The ball will
travel fast and it is easy to hit it to the wrong
side. If in doubt, always hit the ball straight.

Old-fashioned greens – built before 1940
– often sloped from higher at the front to
lower at the back. If they appear dead flat,
take care. The green may in fact be sloping
away from you.

GETTING THE RIGHT LINE

On sloping or undulating greens, correctly reading the line
of shot is all-important – as Liselotte Neumann shows.

REMEMBER
DOWNSLOPE IS
HARD TO SEE

Reading Greens (2)

With experience it isn't just the slope we need to take into account. The grass itself can have quite an effect on the ball. If it is thick and wet, the ball will travel more slowly. If the greens are cut very short, rolled and are very dry the ball will run across them more quickly.

JUDGING PUTTING SPEEDS

Use the practice green before your round, but remember that the greens on the course may be a different speed.

On a green surrounded by trees the grass may be in shadow all day. Look for these to be the slowest greens on the course. Trees to the south of the green, in particular, will leave the green in shadow.

A green in a basin will gather moisture from all around. A ball landing on the green will often stop smartly. The green may be slow to putt.

A plateau green sitting high may drain better than other greens. It is also more likely to dry out in the wind. A ball hitting into the green will easily bounce through. Putts can be quick.

A large tree near a green may throw out roots that draw away the moisture. Look for slightly bare patches, dry areas and putts that may run very quickly.

When grass is mown towards you the mower stripe appears dark. When grass is mown away from you it appears light and shiny. You may find yourself putting into the grass when it is dark and with the grass when it appears shiny. But in certain hot climates you always have to be aware of the way the grass grows. The 'grain' of the grass can have as much bearing as the slope. Again, if the grass looks dark and thick, the grain of the grass is lying towards you, and if the grass looks light and shiny the grain moves away from you. The grain of the grass can be very noticeable alongside the hole, with blades of

PLUMB-BOBBING
Alison Nicholas of England measures the break of her putt by 'plumb-bobbing' – using the putter like a plumb-line to assess the lie of the land.

grass almost over the hole to one side and slightly bare ground on the other side. This shows the grain of the whole green.

The easiest place to see the grain is just off the green, where the grass is longer and probably lies in the same direction. Chipping or putting into the grain gives a slow putt; with the grain, a fast putt.

The grain of the grass will often lie towards the sea or other source of water, towards the sun or away from a mountain. Allow for the grain as you would for a slope and listen carefully to what a local caddie or a professional tells you!

REMEMBER
BEWARE OF GREENS NEAR TREES

Most players spend insufficient time practising putting. Long and medium length putting is mostly about learning to judge distance better.

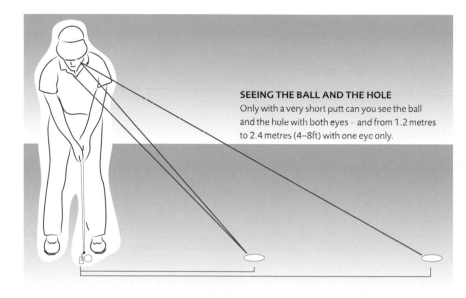

SEEING THE BALL AND THE HOLE
Only with a very short putt can you see the ball and the hole with both eyes – and from 1.2 metres to 2.4 metres (4–8ft) with one eye only.

Practise with six balls from six paces. Set up a box of four tee pegs starting just behind the hole and one putter length square. Club golfers always tend to leave the ball short. Remember, it is easier to make the ball get to the hole than to have the hole come towards you! Give yourself two points for every ball that finishes in the hole and one point for every one that finishes in the box. If you hit six putts from six paces the right distance, then by the law of averages one or two will drop in. The exercise is much harder to do downhill than uphill. Extend the exercises to eight paces and ten paces if you are a would-be champion.

Peg out a piece of string 1 metre (3ft) beyond the hole. Try to make every putt pass the hole without going over the string. Alternatively, lay two clubs down about

1.5 metres (5ft) apart and practise trying to get four balls to finish in this box. It gives you something positive to practise to and you can see your success rate improve.

Don't just practise long putts aimlessly to a hole. Inevitably most of them will miss. If you do this, all you see is failure and it is unlikely to hold your attention.

Put six or ten balls round a green with different lengths and lines. Putt each to the hole and see how many you can get within your putter length. This way, you start learning about your putting and seeing your success rate. To vary your target, put a tee peg down on the green and keep practising to that. Just keep trying to get each ball within a putter length and you will soon be a good long putter.

Set up three balls of the same make but with different numbers. Putt the first one,

TRY THIS EXERCISE
Set up a box of four tee
pegs around the hole,
each about one putter's
length from the hole.
Then try to hit as many
putts into the box as you
can, setting yourself a
target to achieve before
you finish.

putt the second and putt the third without
looking up at each putt. This exercise will
make you aware of your contact. If your
putting stroke is good and your contact
basically sound, all three balls should finish
at much the same length. This teaches you
to feel a good contact.

Lay-backs. For a really testing exercise for
both long putting and short putting, try this
exercise on a nine or eighteen hole putting
green. Play your putt to the hole. If it misses,
always move the ball further away by another
putter length. If you miss again, move it away
a putter length again. This way you
don't simply tap in a series of tiny
putts. It makes you concentrate
on every long putt, with plenty
of practice of the short ones.

REMEMBER
THINK SPEED
AND DISTANCE

One of the worst putting problems is the yips, where the putter literally seems to have a mind of its own, particularly on short putts. This is more likely to happen as one gets older. It can be a problem with the very shortest of putts. The wrists should stay firm with short putting. If you 'yip' putts or your short putting stroke becomes rusty, a change of grip can help.

THE HEAD POSITION
Although you must stand well up and not crouch, your head should be in a horizontal position (left). From here it swivels to see the line of the putt. If the head is too high, it tends to turn and lift, often resulting in problems with direction.

Cross-handed putting

In a cross-handed putting stroke the left arm is extended down the putter, ideally with the left index finger pointing down the shaft. The right hand is at the top and the left beneath. By setting the grip in this way, the back of the left wrist is immediately much straighter and firmer at address.

It can also make the shoulders less dominant, with the right hand and right shoulder less likely to take over. If your short putting stroke is poor, particularly with the clubface twisting through impact, try this grip. Most players who use it move to a conventional grip at around six to eight paces.

If your short putting stroke is poor, make sure you hold the putter firmly enough. Grip the club reasonably firmly and make sure the club hangs slightly above the ground at address. If you hold it too loosely, then the first movement tends to be to gather the weight of the putter and that can set off a jerky stroke. Hanging the putter makes it easier to make a slow, firm stroke.

If you are a poor short putter, remember that one of the problems is that you feel embarrassed about missing. Never feel silly about missing a short putt. After all, even professionals frequently miss them. If playing with strangers, tell them not to be shocked if you miss the odd short one!

Practice swings – yes or no?

A practice swing with a short putt can often confuse your aiming. Never make a practice swing from beside your ball straight towards the hole. When you then step forwards to address the ball the tendency is to aim away to the right. Any practice swing must always be parallel to your putt. Alternatively, if you are

CONQUERING YIPS
Hold the club firmly
and hang it just off
the ground.

IDEAL STANCE
Start with your weight
fairly evenly distributed
on the feet, with the ball
central or just ahead of
centre in the stance.

taking a practice swing just to calm your nerves, do it in a completely different direction. If the practice swing is to give you the feeling of direction – remembering that that is the most important part of short putting – then do it behind the ball or ahead of the ball.

Remember that if you do it between the ball and the hole, you shouldn't touch the ground. Make sure your practice swing doesn't confuse your aiming. If you don't aim correctly then try short putting without any practice swing. It may be causing the aiming difficulties.

Routine

There are three ways to approach a short putt. Firstly, do one or two practice swings. (Don't do more if you get nervous.) Then let go of the putter with one hand, set it behind the ball, re-grip and play your putt.

The second alternative is to do your one or two practice swings, keep hold of the putter, set it to the ball and then play your putt. (Some players find that they can't do this when they get nervous.)

Or thirdly, don't do a practice swing at all. The first routine is probably the most common amongst professional golfers. However, most importantly, if you do a practice swing, always make sure it is parallel to your target.

REMEMBER
KEEP A FIRM
LEFT WRIST

Trouble Shots

When golf was first formally developed as a game – in Scotland, during the 18th and 19th centuries – the courses bore little resemblance to those of today. The game was played over public land – as in places it still is now – with natural hazards and obstacles to negotiate. Not only were walls and ditches part of the game, but players often had to contend with others out enjoying their other various recreations.

It was from these numerous obstacles and hindrances that the 'hazards' of the modern game originated – the bunkers or sandtraps, gullies, streams, ponds and lakes that today characterize golf courses all over the world.

As these hazards are so numerous, and are deliberately positioned by course designers to challenge the golfer, an integral and extremely important part of the modern game involves knowing how to tackle them. For no matter how good a golfer you become, there will be many occasions when your ball falls into a seemingly unplayable lie, into a bunker or simply into the awkward light rough on a slope at the edge of the green. The advice in this chapter will help when the inevitable occurs out on the course.

Johanna Head of England, one of the European Tour's golfing twins.

When you are playing a ball from just off the edge of the green, the easiest thing is to use your putter. Don't think that there is anything amateurish about using your putter rather than chipping. The key is to use the club which works best for you.

You can putt the ball through slightly thicker and wetter grass than most club golfers imagine, but remember that as you strike a ball it first slides, then rolls and then wobbles. If you are playing a very short shot from off the edge of the green, the ball is more likely to get caught up in the grass than playing a longer shot. So, when you can putt, do so. If the grass looks a little too thick to putt through, then chip the ball with a 7

1 Sit the 7 iron up on its toe, sitting up towards you like a putter. Grip well down the grip with your putting grip, standing close to the ball and with your eyes directly over the ball, just as you would with putting. The toe of the club is just slightly into the grass with the heel off the ground. Once you do this in fluffy grass, it doesn't feel awkward.

2 With the club sitting slightly on its toe, position the ball towards the toe of the club. This is the part that will brush the grass. Use the standard putting grip, with the left hand turned round to the left and both thumbs showing. You shouldn't see the logo on the back of your glove. By contrast the wrong grip sees too much of the back of the left hand and lacks firmness for controlling distance.

iron. If you don't have a 7, then use a 6 rather than an 8. The idea of this basic shot is to make a putting stroke with a slightly lofted club so that the shot becomes a putt with a hop. We want to turn the 7 iron into something that feels like a putter. There are three differences. Firstly it is longer, secondly the 7 iron has a round grip rather than a flat grip – so that it will feel different in your hands – and thirdly it sits at a different angle.

In other words, the putter sits up and the 7 iron sits slightly lower. In order to chip well, sit the club up on its toe so that the shaft of the club sits up towards you just like a putter. Use the orthodox putting grip, with your hands the same height off the ground as they would be with your putter. This should put you well down the grip of the club with your right thumb and index finger off the grip and onto the shaft itself.

3 Lean slightly to the left so that the top of the clubshaft is always much closer to the inside of your left wrist than your right one. The weight is slightly on the left foot, with the shoulders level. Unlike putting, the club should just brush the grass very lightly, sending the ball away with a hop. The key with the stroke is not to try to help the ball into the air.

4 The top of the club stays close to the left wrist right the way through to the end of the swing with the left wrist firm. If you incorrectly try to help the ball, the left wrist buckles. Think of hitting slightly down and keeping the ball travelling lower than the club wants to hit it. Resist any feeling of helping it into the air.

REMEMBER
A CHIP IS A PUTT WITH A HOP!

Short Chipping

This little chipping action is just for a shot of up to ten to fifteen paces – a very short one. The more similar you can make it to putting, the better the stroke will be and the more control you will have. Remember that a full 7 iron may hit anything between 80 and 140 metres, depending on your standard. You need to firm the action up to control it for a short distance. Grip the club firmly to keep the shot short.

THE CHIP
Above all, concentrate on keeping the clubshaft and left wrist working together as you bring the clubhead through the ball.

Learn to use your 7 iron and make it feel like
a putter. Line up a row of balls on a green
with a downhill shot. Put the closest 45cm
(18in) away from the hole with 30cm (12in)
between adjacent shots. Set up to the first one
with your 7 iron sitting very much on its toe
and just play a little putting stroke, striking
the ball towards the toe. You will begin to feel
a little bit of spin to the ball and just a tiny

hop. You don't need to brush the green and
you certainly won't damage it. In this way
you learn control and the feeling of the ball
just starting to lift off the ground. It only just
rises. Don't try to help it.

To feel the contact from the toe for a nice
light, gentle contact, line up several balls in a
row. Gradually work along the line, just
brushing the grass and feeling the ball
hopping gently away. Remember to move
your feet between shots!

This is a nice exercise to relate chipping and
putting. Lay your putter down about eight
paces away, putter head facing you. This
becomes the imaginary hole you are aiming to.
Just chip a few balls from off the green towards
your putter. Then lay your 7 iron down just on
the edge of the green and putt a few back
again. Feel how close you stand to the ball with
your putter and see how your eyes are directly
over the ball. Try to reproduce the same sort of
feeling with your 7 iron. Inevitably you will
stand a little further away from the ball, but
the two should feel as similar as possible.

In order to lengthen the chip just a little,
lean very slightly to the left. This de-lofts the
club a fraction and will send it away a little
bit lower and further. But the maximum for

> **EXPERT TIP**
> The top of the club stays close to the left wrist
> right the way through to the end of the swing
> with the left wrist firm. If you incorrectly try to
> help the ball the left wrist buckles. Think of
> hitting slightly down and keeping the ball
> travelling lower than the club wants to hit it.

this shot is only about 15 metres (17 yards) –
it really is only a very short chip. So widen
the stance with your left foot, lean
slightly to the left and always
think of hitting the ball down
and forwards and not trying to
help it into the air.

REMEMBER
HIT FROM THE
TOE FOR
CONTROL

Longer Chipping

To play a slightly longer chip of 15 to 30 metres, you need to alter your technique. The club will sit flatter on the ground, not so much on its toe. The feeling is of leaning slightly ahead of the ball and hitting the ball low and forwards towards the hole.

The feeling should be of geting the ball down onto the ground as early as possible. Don't worry precisely where the ball lands. Just work at judging the overall distance. If the apron near the green is cut smoothly and is dry, you can easily chip at the ball through this fringe.

Take the 7 iron in your right hand and tip it forward slightly so that the club has the loft of a 6 iron. The top of the club has to point to your navel or very slightly left of it, so set your feet a little more ahead of the ball and the ball just behind centre.

Complete the address by leaning slightly to the left, completing your putting grip and tucking your left elbow slightly into the side. The club will now sit flat on its bottom – no longer on the toe. Check the grip. The logo on the left hand glove should still be hidden.

Keep your weight slightly on your left foot and concentrate on hitting the ball low and forward. Brush the ground but don't dig into it. The left wrist should again stay firm. As long as you think down rathr than up, the firmness should remain.

If throwing a ball or rolling a ball towards the target, you would find it very difficult to do so with your feet sideways. The same

follows with this shot. To make it easier, start with your feet parallel to your shot but now turn your left foot out a little so that your knees seem to turn towards the target. This doesn't mean aiming the line across the feet to the left. Simply turn the feet and the knees to make the action easier. Now the legs should just work comfortably towards the target as you swing through.

With a very short chip (pp. 120–1) you should keep the feet perfectly square to lock down the distance. In this shot you need to encourage a little more distance and this foot position will do so.

With all short shots you want to encourage a slightly up and down action. Setting the hands forward and leaning to the left helps you to swing from slightly high to low, making sure you get a good contact. By using a 7 iron and tipping it forward into a

6 iron, it helps you get a contact of ball and then grass. If you simply set up with a 6 iron without pushing the hands forward, the danger would be of hitting the grass before the ball. To make this even easier you eed to ensure that the shoulders sit correctly at address. The golden rule with nearly asll short shots is to keep a high right shoulder. Don't let the right shoulder drop, or you finish up scuffing the ground behind the ball.

To help keep a high right shoulder, go through the process of addressing the ball with the club in the right hand first. Push it forwards. then add the left hand and as you do so feel that you keep the left elbow and the left shoulder down.

For advanced golfers, note that if you out both hands on the club too soon before pushing the hands forward, the right shoulder can get low.

EXPERT TIP
For a long chip from the very front of the green to the very back of the green, use a 6 iron and tip it forward like a 5 or even a 5 iron tipped forward like a 4. Get the ball on the ground as early as possible and get it running smoothly to your target.

THE LONGER CHIP
Turn your left foot out a little and your right foot in a little to encourage the extra distance you require with this chip.

POINT OF CONTACT
Don't take the grass in front of the ball with this shot, but rather aim for a clean contact with low loft, getting the ball back on the ground as early as possible.

REMEMBER
KEEP A
HIGH RIGHT
SHOULDER

Choosing a Sand Wedge

The sand wedge, like the putter and the driver, is a very individual club. It needn't match the rest of your set. A sand wedge is not just for playing shots out of a bunker. It is also the most useful club when you want height and loft around the green. Look for one with plenty of loft. Sand irons vary from 55 to 64 degrees of loft. That is roughly the difference between a 3 iron and a 7 iron. Ideally choose a sand iron with 62 degrees of loft on its face. In this way you can play lofted shots without using a complicated technique.

Look for a sand wedge with between 60–64 degrees of loft with the leading edge of the club forward and not backwards. The club like the one in the centre (opposite) sits comfortably with its face beneath the ball. One like that on the far right is wry-necked and doesn't encourage a good contact.

A sand wedge, like a fairway wood, is designed to bounce on the ground. A pitching wedge, by way of contrast, has a cutting edge, designed to take a divot. Think of the pitching wedge as a club to use for lofted shots when you haven't reached the green. A sand wedge is the correct club for using over bunkers and for lofted shots near the green. The rounded sole of the sand iron will bounce on the ground.

Getting the correct lie to the sand iron is vital. The lie refers to the angle between the club shaft and the vertical. Looking through your set of clubs, the pitching wedge should sit most upright and the sand wedge slightly flatter. If the lie is too upright you will find certain bunker shots and pitch shots difficult. Look for a sand wedge with a lie of

approximately your 7 iron. You will see later that in many shots with a sand iron the knees bend. The correct lie will allow you to do this. For advanced golfers, it will also allow you to open the clubface correctly and comfortably.

For certain bunker shots and advanced shots, we have to open the clubface. This means turning the clubface away to the right. There is more information about this on pages 146 and 154. The rubber (or leather) grips on clubs are usually egg-shaped with the pointed part of the egg at the back of the grip. This helps you to hold the club squarely. With a sand wedge, a perfectly round grip can be easier to use for the specialist shots, when you don't want to hold the clubface squarely, but open.

WRONG
If the club sits too upright, when you try to open the clubface the toe of the club rises and the heel is likely to drag in the sand or the ground.

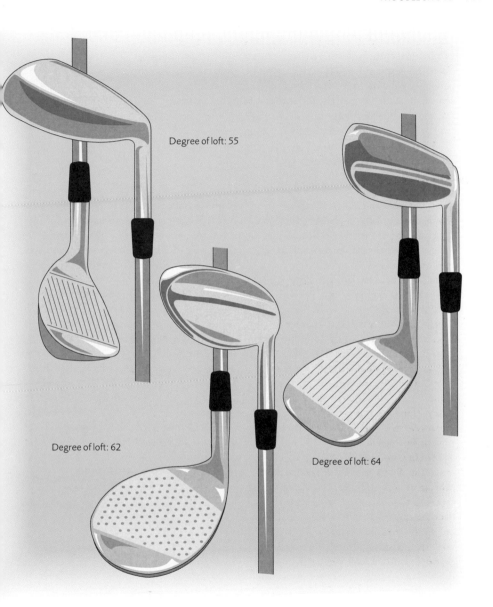

Degree of loft: 55

Degree of loft: 62

Degree of loft: 64

SAND WEDGES

The diagram above shows three different sand wedges, each from two angles. The one in the centre has a rounded leading edge, and is the most inviting shape for getting beneath the ball or opening the face.

REMEMBER
USE 60° TO
64° OF LOFT

Make Friends With Your Sand Wedge

Using a sand wedge around the green is vital. The most
difficult shot for most club golfers is to play a little shot over
a bunker. The sand wedge is the heaviest club in the set. If you
mis-hit the ball it travels too low and too far. It is important
to make friends with your sand wedge and to have confidence
in producing lofted shots.

To acquire confidence with your sand
wedge, practise from 45cm (18in) or so
from the edge of the green. Lay a putter
down on the green no more than four paces
away. Learn to play tiny shots, all finishing
short of your putter. This is much shorter
than shots you would ever really play, but
it teaches good habits.

Use the reverse overlap putting grip with
the left index finger on the outside (see p.
96). If you wear a glove you shouldn't see the
logo on the back of the glove. If you don't
wear a glove you shouldn't see any of the
knuckles on the left hand. The putting grip
adds firmness in the left wrist. The club is
5cm (2in) shorter than the 7 iron; grip near
to the top of the club. Sit the club flat on its
bottom. Remember that the whole idea of
the putting grip is to keep the clubface
working through in a face up position. It also
slows down the wrist action.

To make the ball rise the club must bounce
on the ground as it strikes the ball. Before
each little shot have one or two practice
swings and feel the club bouncing. In this
way you find the bottom of the ball and avoid
hitting it halfway up. To feel the bouncing
contact, sit the ball on a fairly large coin and
concentrate on striking the coin. If you send
the coin away the ball will rise.

The wrong action is of letting the left wrist
collapse in an effort to help the ball into the
air. The correct action is to keep the left wrist
firm and leading. It mustn't stop through
impact. If your left wrist collapses, try, as an
exercise, gripping further down the club. In

this way you can feel the top of the clubshaft
against your left wrist. Hold it there through
impact and beyond to encourage the
bouncing contact and firm left wrist.

Most golfers ruin shots with a sand wedge
by looking up too quickly. The reason for
practising with such a short shot is that the
ball is always within your vision. You can see
the ball out of the corner of your left eye.
Learn to play these very small shots, staying
down without letting the head or eyes move.

Learn to lengthen the shot by pitching over
your putter. Learn the feeling of staying
down. You will know whether you have hit
the ball correctly without looking up. Give
yourself 5 points for a perfect contact and
zero points for a horrible contact. You will
know how good the shot is without moving
your head or eyes. As you lengthen the shot
keep your shoulders level – the high right
shoulder – and simply work at the bouncing
contact and firm finish.

SAND WEDGE SKILLS
Professional women golfers
(like Liselotte Neumann,
shown here in France)
practise sand wedge shots
– from both in and out of
bunkers – for hours in order
to perfect their skills in a
vital part of the game.

REMEMBER
BOUNCE THE
CLUB ON THE
GROUND

Having learnt to make friends with your sand wedge, let's put it into practice. For shots of up to 20 metres maximum, use the putting grip. This helps to keep the wrist firm and the clubface looking upwards for maximum height.

The club is short. Hold it near the end with the putting grip. Grip firmly. At address, the ball should be just ahead of centre in your stance. The better the lie, the further forward you can play it. The clubshaft points to your navel, shoulders as level as possible. Keep the right foot straight ahead or slightly turned in. The essence of the shot is to use the arms, legs and shoulders and to immobilize the wrists. Keep the wrists passive in the backswing, bounce the club on the ground through impact, move through into a followthrough with the clubface looking upwards, back of the left wrist firm, head still and eyes focused on the spot where the ball was.

The putting grip should help you swing the clubface down in the backswing, face up in the throughswing. The backswing should take care of itself. In the throughswing, keep the back of the left wrist upwards, end of the club in contact with the inside of the left wrist and allow the left elbow to stay into the side of your body.

To learn the shot, practise from a slight upslope. The upslope helps to produce height to the shot and gives confidence. Stand with your feet a little closer than you would on a flat lie and feel the clubface working upwards beyond impact. Ideally learn from fluffy grass rather than a bare lie.

The feeling of the shot is to use the legs, arms and shoulders. At address the clubshaft points to your navel. It should point there all the way from start to finish. The grip shouldn't point down to the ground in backswing or throughswing. Have a few practice swings, looking at the grip end of the

THE SHORT PITCH
The short pitch shot is played with wrists firm and elbows as though tied into the body. Move back and through with your shoulders and legs, making sure the backswing and throughswing are the same length.

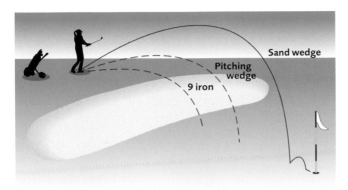

THE RIGHT CLUB

Avoid playing the short pitch with a 9 iron or pitching wedge. If you use a sand wedge, you can land the ball well over the obstacle and nearer the flag.

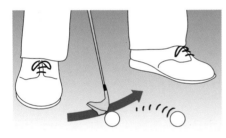

DON'T LIFT

Never try to lift the ball when playing a short pitch shot. The club will catch the top of the ball and top it (above). Make a U-shaped swing, brushing the ground beneath the ball. Think 'down' in order to get the ball up.

SAND AND PITCHING WEDGES

The sand wedge (below right) has more loft than the pitching wedge (below left) and is designed to bounce over the ground rather than cut into it.

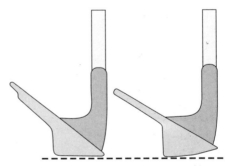

club. Keep it pointing up towards you and within your vision.

As an exercise, hold the club into your navel, hands extended down the shaft, arms straight but clubhead obviously not reaching the ground. Practise swinging back and through with the top of the club into you. This gives the feeling of the legs and shoulders working and the wrists staying passive.

Don't try to help the ball up with your wrists or the clubhead simply rises and

catches the top of the ball. Keep the wrists firm and the left one leading. In short shots think of holding the club more firmly. The club is heavy and you need to grip tightly to keep it moving slowly enough. Don't grip loosely with the idea of being delicate, or the clubhead travels too quickly.

REMEMBER
GRIP FIRMLY
FOR SHORT
SHOTS

Having learnt to putt, chip and play short pitches, you need to decide which shot to play in various situations. Putting is usually the easiest shot, chipping the next easiest and pitching with a wedge by far the most difficult. A thoroughly bad putt from just off the green is usually better than a not quite perfect pitch! So the golden rule for club golfers is to use your putter whenever you can.

It is perfectly possible to putt the ball through fluffy and wet grass. A ball first slides, then rolls and then wobbles as it slows down. It is easier to putt through fluffy grass when going a long distance than a short distance. The speed of a longer shot allows it to slide through or over the grass without getting caught. On a shorter shot the ball is more likely to be trapped in the grass.

A little chip played from the toe of a 7 iron always has a little backspin. If playing a downhill shot, the short chip can be easier to pull to a halt than a putt. The over spin of a putt keeps the ball rolling and may make it

SELECT WITH CARE
Even professionals (like McCurdy and Steinhauer, here at Woburn) have difficulty deciding how to play a particular shot or even which club to use. Club players should not be afraid to ask advice if doubtful.

roll too far. The back spin of a little chip allows you to judge distance better. Conversely, when going uphill a putt will keep rolling and a chip may stop short. So from just off the edge of the green, if both your putting and chipping are good, putt uphill and chip downhill.

Sometimes a chip with a 7 iron just isn't the right shot. You need to assess the ratio of hop to run. On an ordinary chip the ball may, for example, hop one-sixth and run five-sixths of the distance. It depends on the speed of the green. If there is more fluffy grass to negotiate, the ratio may be one-third hop and two-thirds run. In this case you may need to choose an 8 iron, 9 iron, or even a pitching wedge to create the right ratio. Play the shot just like your 7 iron chip – slightly on the toe for a very short shot and with the club sitting flatter, hands forward for a longer shot.

In theory, the correct way of playing a short pitch is to choose where you want the ball to land. There are two dangers to this. Firstly, most people choose a spot that is too short. Secondly, they then pitch short of the spot they have chosen. If you use an 8, 9 iron or wedge to negotiate the grass, choose the right club to land on the green but continue to think of the overall length of the shot rather than your landing spot. If you think of the overall length, you are more likely to keep your head down long enough.

For a short pitch or chip, think of getting the ball in the hole. Focus on hitting it far enough. Take the flag out to focus your attention on where the ball will finish.

The length of swing with a putter or 7 iron is much shorter than with a wedge with far less to go wrong. A poorly struck putt or 7 iron will usually travel the right distance. The wedge requires a longer swing with more to go wrong.

THE CHOICE OF CLUB

It is very important to select the right club when you are faced with an awkward shot from just off the green. Preferably, use a putter (above left), since there is little that can go wrong when using this club. If a putter is unsuitable, the next choice is a 6 or 7 iron (above centre). Play a running shot and judge it in terms of overall length. Look to pitch the ball (above right), only if you cannot use a putter or if you decide that a running shot is unsuitable. The short pitch with a wedge or sand iron is by far the trickiest of these three shots.

REMEMBER
CHIP DOWNHILL, PUTT UPHILL

Negotiating a Bank

When faced with a bank in front of them, most club golfers wrongly assume that the only way to get over it is to use a wedge. But it is not always the easiest and safest way of playing the shot.

Your first choice should be a putter, your second choice a 5, 6 or 7 iron. Your third choice should be a sand wedge. The putter is the easiest and the sand wedge the most difficult of the clubs to play in this situation.

Firstly, look at the grass on the bank ahead of you. If the grass is thick, you may have no alternative but to pitch over it with a sand wedge. If the ground is reasonably bare and the grass fairly short and dry, then the easiest shot is simply a putt. If it looks better than the worst hockey pitch you have ever played on, the ball will probably run through it! Don't worry if the bank is uneven. The ball will probably be thrown to right and left but will work its way to the top of the bank and over it.

If your ball sits in fluffy grass but the grass on the bank is short, then use a 5, 6 or 7 iron and run the ball up the bank.

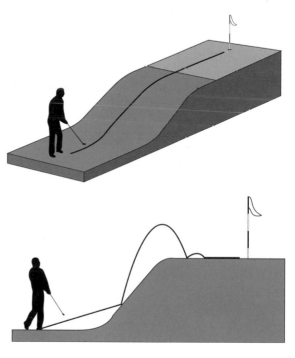

PLAYING OVER A BANK
Use a putter whenever possible (above, top). If the grass is at all fluffy, or you are faced with a longer shot, run the ball with a 5 or 6 iron. If the bank is steep, but smooth, and the flag is just over it, you can try punching the ball at the bank with a 4 iron (above, bottom). It should pop up and over.

This is also the correct shot if the ground is bare and the shot looks too long for using your putter.

To run the ball up the bank you need to use a 5, 6 or 7 iron and to tip the club forward like a 4 iron so that it runs low and scuttles up the bank. Hold whichever club you choose in your right hand and tip it forward to the loft of a 4 iron. If less than

40 metres (45 yards) or so, use a putting grip. Use a wide stance and lean to the left so the top of the club points to your navel or just left of it. Keep the shoulders level. Keep the hands leading and think of punching the ball low so that it gets onto the ground and bounces at least twice as it runs up the bank.

The reason for tipping the club forward from its standard loft is to ensure that you hit

PLAY THE RIGHT CLUB
Whenever the lie allows, and you are not too far from the green, play your putter. Otherwise, use a mid iron, as here, in preference to a sand wedge.

PUNCH IT FORWARDS
With this shot using a 7 iron, keep the hands leading all the way through the stroke, punching the ball forwards and keeping the ball low.

the ball first and then the ground after it. Don't just use a 4 iron. Tip the club forward for a ball-ground contact. The 5 iron is often easier to use but the shaft can feel uncomfortably long for women golfers. The 7 iron is more manageable in length but needs to be tipped forward more.

Running a ball with a 5, 6 or 7 iron is particularly useful when the flag is just over the top of the bank. There may be very little landing room for a sand wedge shot and the running shot is easier to control.

You need to consider carefully the way the ball sits. Different lies require different shots. The three shots from a divot hole, an ordinary lie and a tuft of grass require a different approach. Most players wrongly try to putt from the tuft of grass and use a wedge from the divot hole. With the ball sitting in a divot you can only strike the back of the ball.

You can't find the bottom of the ball with a sand wedge unless you are hitting a longer shot and going to take an even larger divot. If the ball sits in a divot hole, use a putter. The putter will meet the back of the ball. The ball will jump out of the hole and run forwards. Use an ordinary swing with your putter, perhaps using a little more wrist than normal. You'll be surprised how easily the ball jumps and runs on its way. It can be easier putting from a divot than from a good lie. If the shot looks too long for your putter, then run it with a 5, 6 or 7 iron. If you wrongly use your sand wedge, the swing is much longer than with either of the other two clubs, and you will simply strike the back of the ball and thin it far too far. Only use your sand wedge from a good, tufty lie when you can find the bottom of the ball with ease.

REMEMBER PUTT WHENEVER POSSIBLE

Running and Punch Shots

The easiest way of approaching a green from 40 or 50 metres short of it is to run the ball in with a 7 iron. A 7 iron is a forgiving club. You can play rotten shots with a 7 iron that still work! If the ground is reasonably dry and the grass cut, simply use a 7 iron and play a shot like a hockey shot. Up to 30 or 40 paces from the green, use your reverse overlap putting grip to keep the wrists firm and the shot short enough. With a longer shot revert to you ordinary grip.

Use a wide stance, ball central or just ahead of centre, and lean slightly to the left. The backswing should feel to be very short, right arm folding but wrists staying firm. As you swing on through, transfer your weight with the top half of your body to the left, strike the ball then the turf and finish with the club pointing out towards your target. The backswing always needs to feel much shorter than it looks. Rather like swinging a hockey stick, a swing that feels waist height is often above the shoulders. So have a practice swing where you stop to feel

the distance. Again, like hitting out from under trees you may have two or three practice swings below the tree branch but as soon as you swing, the club travels further.

To make the shot easier, turn your feet and knees towards the target. Turn the right foot in a little and the left foot out a little so that your knees seem to go towards the target. This will help you shorten the backswing and make the throughswing on-target.

In the finish of the swing the clubface should be in a toe-up position. Right arm folds in the backswing, left arm folds in the

throughswing. The top half of your body should move forward towards the target, left upper arm staying into your side and not stretching away. Think of the shot as being like an inverted saucer. The swing is saucer shaped – low in the backswing and low in the throughswing.

At the end of the swing the left arm should bend but the wrist should be firm. There should almost be a straight line from left elbow to clubhead. The action isn't stiff in the left arm and a break in the wrist.

At the end of the swing the club should finish toe-up with a real sense of direction towards your target. Hold your finish until the ball stops rolling. The clubhead will seem to finish slightly left of target. Remember, your body and club aim down the left of a pair of 'railway lines' and the ball travels off down the right one. This shot is useful when the ground is firm. It is difficult to tell whether a wedge shot will stop on landing or run on landing. We know this shot will run. It is useful in the wind, whether against or across. It is also useful for punching out between or beneath trees – particularly in mixed foursomes! Always keep the backswing short enough so that you feel that you can accelerate.

When playing on to a two-tier green, aim to run the ball in rather than pitching it. A wedge shot pitching on the bottom layer doesn't run up the green. If pitching on the top layer it kicks through. A running short landing short of the green will scuttle its way onto the top layer.

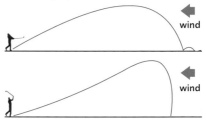

THE PUNCH SHOT
The punch shot is aimed at keeping the ball 'driving' forward and is useful for penetrating a headwind (see above).

Target direction

PLAYING THE SHOT
Use anything from a 3 iron to a pitching wedge to play this shot, keeping the ball back in the stance, with the clubface square and your hands forward. Take a firm backswing and a short, punchy finish.

REMEMBER
KEEP THE BACKSWING SHORT ENOUGH

Longer Pitching

The running shot is useful from 30 to 90 metres when there is nothing in the way. It is a surprisingly easy shot to control and many women are surprised just how far they can run a ball with a 7 iron. But when you haven't reached the green and still have an obstacle to go over – whether it's a pond or a bunker – you need to play a more lofted shot with a 9 iron, pitching wedge or sand wedge. The technique is much the same as that for the running shot from the previous pages. Learn the shot first with a pitching wedge if you have one, 9 iron if you haven't.

THE LONG PITCH
With the long pitch (below), limit the backswing to allow you to accelerate through the ball to a controlled finish. Never flick or loosen your wrists in the throughswing.

The pitching wedge sits more upright than the 7 iron. This should automatically make the swing more up-down-up. It will be more up-down-up rather than wide and shallow.

Use a wide stance, just as with the running shot, turning the left foot out a little and the right foot in. Feel that the backswing is short, with passive wrists. Again, as with the running shot, the swing will go much further than you think. Feel your swing back below shoulder height and minimize the wrist break.

As you strike the ball you need to take the ball and then a divot beyond it.

At the finish of the swing your weight should transfer to your left side, making a punchy finish with the club at 1 or 2 o'clock on an imaginary clock face. The toe of the club should be toe upwards. There should be an almost straight line from left elbow to clubhead, left arm and upper body staying together, left arm bending and left wrist firm. At the end of the swing the head should move to the left towards the target but with the eyes staying looking down as long as possible.

EXPERT TIP
The shot can be played with a 9 iron, pitching wedge or sand wedge. The different clubs progressively give shorter distances. In each case, trust the loft of the club and don't try to help the ball up.

LONGER AND ADVANCED PITCHING

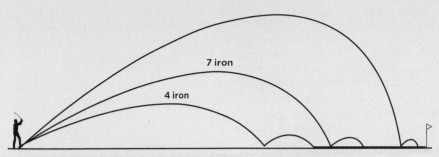

7 iron

4 iron

ADAPTATION OF THE SHOT

The long pitch can be adapted using a 4 iron or 7 iron to produce lower, punched shots than are achievable with a pitching wedge.

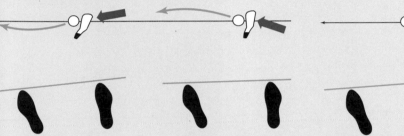

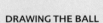

CUTTING THE BALL IN

To cut the ball in (above), set the clubface slightly open at address and aim the stance left.

DRAWING THE BALL

To draw the ball (above), close the clubface noticeably left and attack the ball from the inside.

STANCE

With long pitching and punch shots, play the ball back in the stance. Turn the line of the feet left until this brings the shot on target.

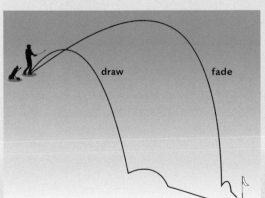

draw

fade

FADE AND DRAW

With practice you will learn to fade and draw your long pitches, which is particularly useful when playing with a cross wind.

REMEMBER
MAKE A FIRM,
PUNCHY
FINISH

Taking a Divot

The running shot with a 7 iron is more forgiving and easier than a pitch. If you slightly mis-hit the ball it still travels the correct distance. If you mis-hit a longer pitch with a wedge the ball travels too low, lands in the pond or bunker you are trying to negotiate or simply runs too far. The key to playing good pitch shots is to be able to take the ball and then a divot. This means that the ball is hit slightly on the downswing, squeezing the ball up and away into the air.

The key movement to being able to take a divot is to allow the top half of the body to move towards the target through and beyond impact. It isn't head still, hips forward. Correctly the top half of the body and head move toward the target. Learn to take a small divot when playing a running shot with a 7 iron. If you don't, the shot is still a success but it trains the correct movement.

With a wedge, learn the feeling of making a ball-divot contact. Think of your head starting opposite the ball but your head finishing opposite your left foot. The top half of the body moves forward and this should correspond with taking the divot. Keep your eyes looking down and count to three before looking up.

Many women dislike the feeling of taking a divot. Partly there is a fear of hurting yourself. But part of the fear is that taking a divot is untidy. Men usually find taking a divot very easy. Women find it difficult. If you don't like damaging the ground, practise hitting weeds. Seriously, grass is good and weeds are bad. Punch them away, moving your head to the left.

To take a divot, remember that you hit down and not under. The right shoulder must stay high and not low. The right shoulder stays high and it correctly moves through and round, not down and under. Learn to play the shots with the ball positioned just ahead of centre, transferring

THE POINT OF IMPACT
Remember, hit the ball and then the divot. Don't just bury the clubhead in the ground, but instead make sure that it passes through and beyond the divot.

the weight with the top half of your body. Don't just bury the club in the ground but allow the club to go into the ground and through and out the other side.

Remember that these shots are not like hitting a tennis ball. You cannot get beneath the ball. The instinct for many tennis players is to let the right hand wrongly slip underneath the club and try to scoop the ball up. Do just the reverse. Keep the right hand well over and think of hitting down and through the ball and ground.

PLAYING GOOD PITCH SHOTS

If you take a divot as you play your pitch shot, it means that you have been successful in hitting slightly on the downswing, squeezing the ball out from your clubhead and away into the air. This indicates an efficient and well-executed shot that will generally end up where you intended it to go.

REMEMBER
HIT THE BALL,
THEN THE
DIVOT

Shortening the Pitch

Practise playing a long pitch with whatever length you feel comfortable. With a pitching wedge you may achieve 40 or 80 metres. First learn to make a good contact. You then have to adjust the swing to hit different lengths of shots. The difficulty is to make shorter shots than you feel comfortable with.

The typical club golfer's action of playing a shorter shot is to make a long backswing and decelerate. Correctly the backswing must be short enough to allow you to accelerate.

To shorten your shot from your most comfortable distance, grip down the club a few centimetres, reduce the length of the backswing and accelerate firmly through the ball into a punchy finish.

Try to throw a golf ball with an underarm throw 30 or 40 metres. It is a long way. That is how a pitch shot should feel. The

backswing must be short enough to allow you the feeling of accelerating and hitting really hard through impact.

When you want to play a shorter shot still, grip the club really firmly and concentrate on the clubface. Learn to swing the clubface through into a face-up position. This means that the back of the left hand stays on top and the left wrist stays really firm. Have two or three practice swings, watching the face of the club and learning to hold it up. This is how professionals get backspin onto their

shots. Instead of the club swinging toe-up, which keeps the ball moving forwards and perhaps running, 'pros' usually swing into a face-up position, which gives the ball more backspin and bite when landing.

To shorten your shot even more, use your sand wedge. Grip firmly and eventually change down to your putting grip for added control. The shorter the shot you want, the firmer and tighter the grip should be.

SHORTENING FOR RECOVERY
If you are in trouble off the edge of the fairway, reduce your pitch and follow the golden rule of playing a recovery shot by the shortest route back to the fairway.

EXPERT TIP
Practise different lengths of shots. Play to three different targets, perhaps 20, 40 and 60 metres away, and get the feeling of the different shots. The key is to cut that backswing down, grip tightly enough and always accelerate through the ball with a ball divot contact. Let the head move left but the eyes stay focused on the spot where the ball was.

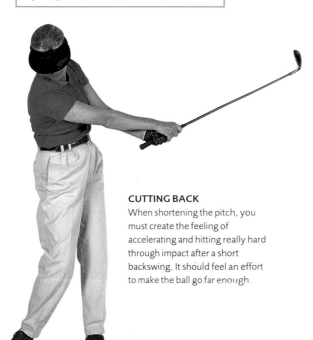

CUTTING BACK
When shortening the pitch, you must create the feeling of accelerating and hitting really hard through impact after a short backswing. It should feel an effort to make the ball go far enough.

'PRO' STYLE
If you are a more advanced golfer, make the clubhead swing face-up for more bite and backspin – as Sweden's Helen Alfredsson demonstrates here.

REMEMBER ALWAYS ACCELERATE

Advanced Pitching

This section is for the low handicap golfer and aspiring champion. There are several other advanced shots needed in certain conditions for approaching the green. In most cases the shots involve adding spin to the shot.

Drawing a running shot.
When playing in windy conditions with the wind from left to right, it can be useful to play a shot that spins from right to left. Learning to draw the ball from right to left with a running shot also helps advanced players to produce the same spin with a driver or other long shot. Drawing a ball with a running shot is like playing topspin with a table tennis bat. The feeling is of hitting the ball from in-to-out and imparting spin. Follow the technique of the running shot on p. 136, using a 5, 6 or 7 iron. Don't change your grip. Address the ball towards the toe of the club. In the takeaway, feel that the clubface stays looking at the target, in other words staying 'hooded' rather than toe-up. Through impact, move in-to-out across the back of the ball as though wiping sidespin onto the ball in table tennis. The clubface literally moves from toe towards heel as it strikes the ball. Don't expect the ball to bend dramatically from right to left. The shot may only be 50 to 100 metres. But it will have right-to-left spin to hold into a cross wind.

Cutting the ball with a running shot.
Playing into a right-to-left wind we can use the opposite effect and play a shot that spins from left to right. In this case the ball goes away with added height. A 5 or 6 iron will produce the normal height of a 7 or 8 iron punch shot.

PITCHING LIKE A 'PRO'
As you become a more proficient golfer, you will learn how to impart spin on just about all your shots, in the same way as professional golfers. It is easier to learn draw and fade with a driver from the tee initially (see pp.164–5), but with plenty of practice and good natural ability, drawing, fading and cutting shots all become options with long, medium and short irons.

Address the ball with the grip firm and the clubface slightly open. Aim your feet slightly left of target to allow for spin to the right. Make your ordinary running shot backswing. Through impact lead very much with the back of the left hand, holding the clubface open and keeping the clubface facing the target beyond impact. Don't think of swinging out-to-in. But through impact feel the clubface pulling slightly inwards across the ball to add slice spin. If you need to think about it, the left elbow pulls away across the side of the body.

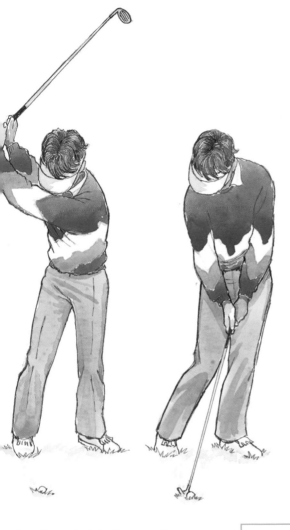

Fading a pitch shot. This is particularly useful to make the ball take up backspin and stop quickly. Don't hold the clubface open at address or you may get unwanted height. Just before impact, have the feeling of pulling the clubface across the ball to add sidespin. Feel the back of the left hand stays firm, the left elbow slides slightly across your body and the clubface stays looking at the target beyond impact, face forwards and up, not toe-up.

The cut shot. To play a high, cut up shot with a sand wedge, lay the clubface open by turning the toe of the club out and lowering your hands. The top of the clubshaft still points to your navel so square yourself up. Use a wide stance and bend your knees. Only play this shot if the ball sits well on plenty of grass.

Drawing a pitch. To draw a pitch shot into a green for perhaps 40–90 metres, follow the running shot technique, using a 9 iron or pitching wedge. Make sure the toe of the club finishes toe-up in the followthrough or even slightly face down. This keeps the ball moving through the air with a penetrating shot. It will hold into a cross wind or keep moving forward when the flag is at the back of the green. In a cross wind, hold the clubface of your pitching wedge very closed at address, turning the toe well in to counteract the effect of the wind.

EXPERT TIP

As an exercise for holding the face open, use a 7 iron from a very grassy lie. Open the face quite dramatically, bend your knees, keep the clubshaft pointing to the middle of yourself, and hold the face open. Master this, and cut shots and bunker shots with a sand wedge will hold no fears.

REMEMBER
FEEL THE
CLUBFACE

Basic Bunker Shots

Learn to play a simple bunker shot of perhaps 12 to 15 paces from a bunker beside a green. Use a sand wedge with plenty of loft (pp. 126–7).

At address, use a square clubface (not opened or turned out), a wide stance, play the ball just ahead of centre with the clubshaft pointing towards your navel, not with the hands forward. Hold at the top of the club; don't grip further down. Most importantly, leave a 5cm (2in) gap between the clubface and the ball and focus your eyes on the spot in the sand behind the ball. Make a threequarter backswing – don't be too concerned about this. Look at the sand and concentrate on hitting the sand and the ball forwards onto the green. Make a threequarter-length finish and keep the grip firm. The whole concept of the shot is to hit the sand forwards onto the green.

Let the top half of your body move forwards towards the target. Most golfers wrongly fall backwards in an attempt to help the ball up and either hit the sand behind the ball or take no sand at all. The correct feeling should be of hitting the sand forwards onto the green.

The rules don't allow you to have a practice swing in a bunker and to take sand. But to learn the shot, make several practice swings, simply concentrating on the sand and trying to hit it forwards.

Practise with a yellow or orange ball. Imagine this is the yoke of your fried egg. With your finger, draw in the white of the fried egg. Imagine hitting the whole of the fried egg out onto the green without popping the yoke! This will teach you to focus on the sand and to take your sand at the right place.

To feel the forward movement of the upper body, try this exercise. Draw one line in the sand 5cm (2in) behind the ball and another 12.5cm (5in) beyond it. Hold the clubhead above the line behind the ball. Your head starts opposite this line. By the finish of the swing the club should take the sand and the ball, and your head should finish opposite the other line. Your head and body move forward to hit the sand forwards.

USING A PUTTER IN A BUNKER
Occasionally you may be able to use a putter in a shallow bunker. The depth of contact is crucial. Keep the head of the putter well above the sand and concentrate on a neat strike on the back of the ball.

HIT THE SAND
Don't be afraid to take plenty of sand with your shot. The whole concept is to hit sand forwards onto the green to ensure a good contact with the ball. Mayumi Hirasi does so at McDonald's LPGA championship in the US.

FINESSE BUNKER SHOTS
The good player can add a little wrist action to playing low, flat shots out of bunkers onto the green.

REMEMBER
LOOK AT THE SAND BEHIND THE BALL

Basic Bunker Shots (2)

The key to playing good bunker shots near the green is to take sand. You need to take the right amount of sand as accurately as possible. If you listen to the contact with a bunker shot you should hear the club take the sand but not strike the ball itself.

To make your striking of the sand as accurate as possible, keep your shoulders level at address. Remember the golden rule of keeping a high right shoulder in the short game. With the right shoulder held high and the shoulders level, the backswing should feel to be an up and down action, without having to use the wrists. This makes it as easy as possible to enter the sand 5cm (2in) or so behind the ball. But still keep in mind that you have to hit the sand forwards onto the green and not simply dig into it.

If you have any problems with your grip it is likely to be at its worst with bunker shots! Make sure your right hand never slips underneath the club as though trying to scoop the ball up and out. All this will do is to close the clubface and reduce the height.

As in all short shots, the grip should be really firm. This keeps the clubhead moving slowly. Try using the reverse overlap putting grip (p. 96). Make sure the left hand is turned well round to the left so you don't see the logo on your glove. This firms up the left hand and will help you keep the clubhead moving slowly and the clubface looking face-up beyond impact. It tends to take out the speed of unwanted wrist action.

Remember, a loose action produces long shots – and you don't want that in a bunker. A stiff action produces short shots. That is what we do want.

Keep swinging slowly in the bunker to make the club travel through the sand. If you develop too much speed, the clubhead gets caught. It would be quite easy to push a pencil slowly and easily through the sand.

By contrast, if you fired a bullet at it the sand would grab it and stop it. A slow swing travels through the sand more easily than a quick, chopping action.

To practise the feeling of a slow swing for a bunker shot, take hold of three clubs altogether – say your 9, pitching wedge and sand wedge. Just hold them the best you can. Now try to make a swing and feel how slowly you have to move them to keep any sort of control. This is the feeling of the timing of a bunker shot. Make it feel ridiculously slow. It will still be a lot quicker than you imagine!

Practise your bunker shots from a good lie to encourage confidence and a good technique before you are faced with less forgiving lies out on the course.

EXPERT BUNKER PLAY
Karrie Webb of Australia, playing a bunker shot during a record round of 63 at the British Women's Open at Sunningdale, England.

REMEMBER
HIT THE SAND
FORWARDS!

Unfortunately we don't always get a perfect lie in a bunker. But learn your basic technique from a good lie and this will give you confidence.

A buried ball. This is not a difficult shot. Most club golfers over-hit with short bunker shots. You certainly won't over-hit with this one! Set up to the ball with a wide stance and a square or slightly closed clubface. Leave a 2.5cm (1in) gap between the club and the ball. Look at the sand just behind the ball and beat down and forwards into it as hard as you can. It requires brute force to get this shot out. Followthrough as well as you can and don't look up.

UNDER THE BUNKER FACE
When playing a ball from under the bunker face, lean into the bank. Concentrate on the back of the ball and hit firmly into it to send the ball up into the air.

A ball in a footprint is much harder to play. If you mis-hit this it can travel much too far. Address the ball with a square clubface and your normal 5cm (2in) gap between club and ball. The trick is to get the right shoulder as high as possible, bending your left arm and stretching your right side. This allows the backswing to be an up-and-down action with maximum chance of getting into the sand at the right place. Treat the shot with caution, make the swing slow and steady and focus on hitting the sand and ball forwards.

The ball under the face of the bunker (see illustration above). The upslope acts as a launch pad to help your ball up and out. The key is to take your stance without grounding your club and to get your feet in the correct position first time. Stand far enough away from the ball and completely upright. Make sure you get a firm footing on your right foot to hoist yourself up. Don't let the left knee and leg get in the way of your swing. Use a square clubface. The upslope is going to give you plenty of height. Look beneath and behind the ball and swing backwards and forwards into the sand. Don't expect to follow through. Just chop into it and the ball should pop up. Keep your head and eyes perfectly still. Don't look at your shot, or you will get a face full of sand. You will always see 'pros' playing this shot and then turning away from it. The sand should go down your collar and not in your eyes!

STEEP BUNKER FACES
When the bunker face is very steep, you may have to settle on your left knee, with your right foot in the sand. Use a lower grip and put your weight on the left side.

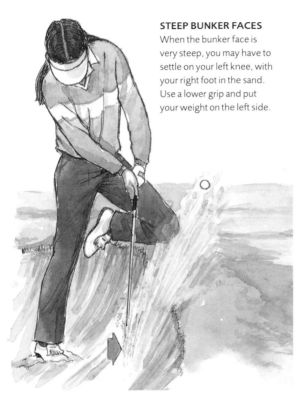

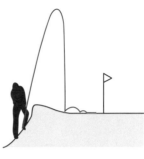

HIT IT HARD!
It does not matter how hard you hit the ball from a steep slope, since it will pop up more or less vertically and hopefully land on top of the bank and kick forward.

If your ball is in the bunker and you have to stand outside it, use a very wide stance and knock your knees inwards so you can get a clear swing at the ball. Keep the ball towards the toe of the club, look at the sand behind the ball and try to play your ordinary bunker shot.
Frozen or compacted sand. Use a square clubface. Treat the shot like a tiny pitch from grass. Use your sand wedge, a putting grip, look at the ball itself and make a very small, slow swing making a contact with the sand at the very spot on which it sits. Keep your grip

firm and keep the action tight and slow.
To putt from a bunker. If the sand is smooth in front of you and there is no lip, a putt can be the easiest shot. Look at the ball itself and not the sand and concentrate on hitting it as cleanly as possible from the top of the sand without making contact with it. Watch the ball well. As with many of the shots described previously, imagine a nail or drawing pin in the back of the ball and make a perfectly horizontal strike.

REMEMBER
TAKE THE SIMPLEST ROUTE OUT

Using a square clubface and a sand iron with 60–64 degrees of loft will get you out of anything you can see out of. The aim for club golfers should be to get the ball out onto the green every time without being overly ambitious. A more advanced shot involves opening the clubface for added height and backswing. You should only attempt these from a good lie in a well-raked bunker.

To feel the correct action of opening the clubface, turn the toe of the club out very slightly, about 1cm (½in). Now have some practice swings in the sand (or on grass) and you should feel the bottom of the sand wedge making a bouncing contact. To play a good, open-faced bunker shot, you need to feel the clubhead bouncing in the sand and to be very aware of the bottom of the clubhead. This will help you add height and backspin.

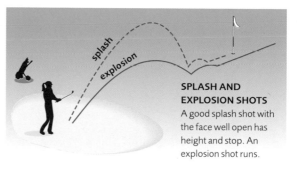

SPLASH AND EXPLOSION SHOTS
A good splash shot with the face well open has height and stop. An explosion shot runs.

At address, turn the clubface out very slightly and then grip the club. As you turn the face out make sure you keep the ball towards the toe of the club. It probably won't be as near the toe as you imagine. Secondly, it may feel awkward in your hands. Open the clubface first and then grip. The egg-shaped part of your rubber grip will feel strange in your fingers. Trust it. Remember the two golden rules of the short game. Firstly the clubshaft points to your navel. Secondly the right shoulder needs to be high.

As you play the shot, concentrate on bouncing the clubface into the sand, still looking 5cm (2in) behind the ball. The clubface should stay open, face upwards beyond impact. Allow your left arm to bend away to your side, left elbow rubbing across you, back of the left hand and clubface upwards. The ball should pop up with greater height and will probably drift away to the left. Don't worry too much about the direction of the shot. Initially expect the ball to finish 1.5 or 1.83 metres (5 or 6ft) right of target. Only when you are confident with adding some height and backspin to the shot should you think about the direction.

We talk about opening the stance in a bunker shot. This simply means turning the feet and stance round to the left to allow for the ball to drift away to the right. It might also add a little more sidespin. To open the stance, remember that the top of the club must still point to your navel. Turn the whole stance round in a circle. Hold at the end of the club; don't grip down it. Keep the stance wide, hands low and knees bent.

To practise the shot, experienced golfers should tee the ball on a high tee peg on grass or a really good lie on the sand. Lay the clubface open and try to slide the clubhead beneath the ball, taking the tee peg and seeing the ball drop to the ground. Imagine the ball has little legs and you are trying to cut them from beneath it.

PLAYING THE EXPLOSION SHOT

To play this shot from a bad lie in the sand, use a square clubface with the ball back in the stance. Look 2.5cm (1in) behind the ball and punch through on the left foot.

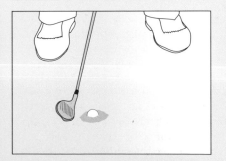

SPLASH SHOT SET UP

With the splash shot, the ball is forward in the stance and the clubface and stance are open.

EXPLOSION SHOT SET UP

With the explosion shot, the clubface is square and the ball further back in the stance.

REMEMBER
BOUNCE THE SOLE OF YOUR CLUBHEAD

Varying Your Distance

To vary your distance you need to be able to control one set distance in the first place! Learn a basic bunker shot of about 12 paces. This should get you out of any bunker around the green and be short enough not to run through the other side.

For a very short shot of say 8 metres (9 yards), grip very firmly, look at the sand 5cm (2in) behind the ball as normal, turn the clubface out slightly to feel the bouncing sole of the club, make a short slow backswing and allow yourself to accelerate smoothly through the sand. You must still get the sand forwards onto the green. The danger of this is of decelerating. Concentrate on getting out.

20 to 25 metres (22–27 yards) can be an awkward length and is one that even 'pros' can find hard to control. Use a square clubface, a 2.5cm (1in) gap between the club and the ball (instead of 5cm/2in). Look closer to the ball than you would with an ordinary shot. Take a full, slow swing and concentrate on taking a far smaller scoop of sand than your normal 'fried egg'.

When you want a long distance with a bunker shot, you need to assess the lie. If the ball sits completely on top of the sand treat the shot like an ordinary fairway shot, taking the ball as cleanly as possible. Stand on top of the sand, without shuffling your feet in at all. Hold the clubhead directly at the back of the ball and as low to the sand as possible without of course touching it. Look slightly higher up on the ball than you might for a normal fairway shot, to ensure that you really do hit it cleanly. You don't want any contact with the sand or you take off distance.

If you want length from a bunker shot and the ball is slightly below the sand, you need a different approach. Now your contact on the ball must be the equivalent of taking the ball and then a divot beyond it. In this case, of course, it is ball and then sand. Play the ball centrally in your stance, right shoulder high,

GETTING OUT
First, always ensure you get out of the bunker (as Lisa Hackney demonstrates here). Then, learn how to control the weight and length of your shot.

hands slightly forward. This will help you hit the ball first and the sand beyond. The key is not to take any sand before making contact.

If the ball sits well and there is little or no bank in front of you, it is perfectly possible to use a 5 wood or 7 wood. Hold the clubface squarely and as close to the ball and sand as you dare without touching either. Don't tip the hands forward or the front edge of the club digs into the sand. Keep the clubface square so that if you do inadvertently catch the sand just behind the ball the sole of the club bounces through and gives you a good contact. Focus your eyes on the back of the ball. Look slightly higher on the ball than you would normally. This ensures that the contact is as clean and sand-free as possible.

HITTING DIFFERENT DISTANCES

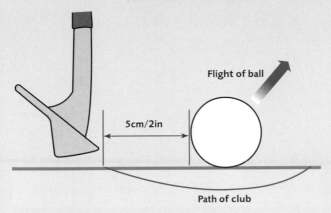

Flight of ball

5cm/2in

Path of club

SHORT BUNKER SHOTS

When aiming to hit about 8 metres (9 yards), shorten the swing and slow it down. Aim about 5cm (2in) behind the ball and do not touch the sand with your clubhead.

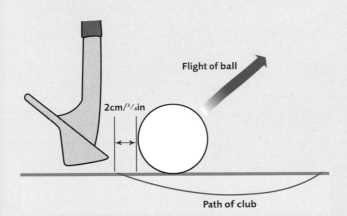

Flight of ball

2cm/³⁄₄in

Path of club

MEDIUM BUNKER SHOTS

When going for about 20 or 25 metres (22 to 27 yards), use a splash shot with a square rather than open clubface. Look closer to the ball – about 2cm (³⁄₄in) – and take less sand.

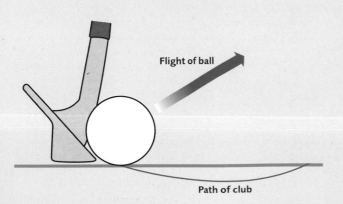

Flight of ball

Path of club

LONG BUNKER SHOTS

With a long bunker shot from a perfect lie, just aim to hit the ball cleanly. From a poorer lie, hit ball and then sand. Take enough loft to negotiate any lip.

REMEMBER THE CONTACT IS ALL-IMPORTANT

Downhill Shots

Downhill shots are always difficult. The first problem is that the ground gets in the way before your make contact with the ball.

If you make the mistake of taking your ordinary address position, you are likely to hit the ground behind the ball and probably miss it altogether.

In any downhill shot you need to make your shoulders follow the slope so that you can swing up and down the slope. To do this you need a very wide stance, all your weight on your left leg, right shoulder as high as possible. Obviously this feels awkward. Your body doesn't want to stand in that way. A downhill shot has the widest stance of any shot you play. Keep the right foot straight ahead, right shoulder high. The ball will look central to you as you look at it but will be behind centre in the stance. The clubshaft points to your navel. As you swing through impact concentrate on following through down the slope, allow the clubshaft to finish on your left shoulder and with your weight over your left leg. In this way you can make a perfectly good contact, without the ground getting in the way before you strike the ball.

The second problem with a downhill shot is that the slope takes off loft. If you use a 7 iron from a steep slope, it may fly low like a 3 iron. Take plenty of loft. Abandon your 3, 4

and 5 irons and your 3 and 5 woods. They won't get airborne. If you make a good contact the ball flies lower and further than normal. Expect it to drift away to the right, so aim left of your target to allow for this.

With a downhill shot around the green, follow the same principle. Use your sand wedge and a putting grip to firm up your wrists. Use a very wide stance, right foot straight in front, right shoulder as high as possible and your weight on your left leg. Make a very short, controlled swing. The ball will probably travel lower and further than you imagine. The putting grip helps curb the distance. If playing over a bunker from this lie, concentrate on hitting down beyond impact and keeping your head and eyes down for a count of three. Expect the ball to run on landing. Only accomplished players should open the clubface to counteract .

With a downhill chip, vary the club you use to allow for the run – a sand wedge to the closest point, a pitching wedge to the middle of the green and a 9 iron to the other end. Keep the swing short, firm and slow.

From a downhill lie near the green you either need plenty of loft, or use the putter.

SHORT DOWNHILL SHOTS
With a short shot from a downslope the ball will fly lower than normal, so use a club with plenty of loft – the sand wedge. Allow the ball to run much more than normal on landing.

DOWNHILL SHOTS TECHNIQUE

Play the ball well back in the stance with the clubface open and your right shoulder high. Use a wide stance.

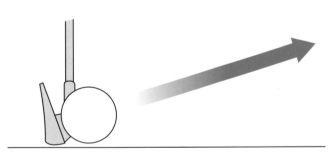

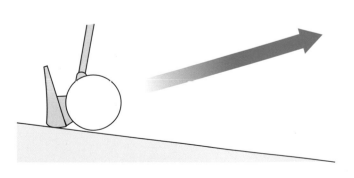

LOFT REDUCTION

A downslope reduces the effective loft of the club. It will turn a 6 iron into a 4 iron loft and make long irons and fairway woods very difficult to use.

REMEMBER
WIDE STANCE,
SHOULDERS
FOLLOW THE
SLOPE

Uphill Shots

Uphill shots are generally much easier to play than downhill shots. Now the ground only gets in the way after you have made contact with the ball. A downhill lie keeps the ball down and is generally more difficult. With an upslope, the ball tends to come up easily and therefore gives confidence. With a downhill lie there is only one method of playing the shot – leaning down the slope. With an uphill lie there are two methods of approach.

One method with an uphill lie is to use the same principle as with the downslope. Lean out from the slope with your shoulders following the slope. Keep your feet a normal width or possibly slightly wider than normal. Try a practice swing from this lie. You realize

your weight hangs back and at the end of the swing your weight is likely to remain on your right foot. If you play the shot this way, place the ball just ahead of centre, swing down the slope and then up the slope through and beyond impact. The ball will travel high and

LONG WOOD SHOTS
For long uphill shots with a wood, lean out from the slope and swing down and up it (left).

IRON SHOTS
For an uphill iron shot, lean into the slope and keep your weight on your left foot throughout. Sway to the left on impact (right).

drift away to the left. Aim to the right toallow for this.

The second method of playing from an upslope is to use an extremely narrow stance, with your feet no more than 15cm (6in) apart. As you followthrough, force yourself to climb up on to your left leg and to make sure that your right foot really can get through onto the tips of the toes. The stance needs to be uncomfortably narrow to allow this to happen. If you can convince yourself to play an upslope shot with this method, the ball will probably travel with a little extra height but you should be able to keep it flying straight. If the slope is steep, you may feel you cannot use this method, for the club will inevitably dig into the ground beyond impact. Try both methods and see which you prefer. In any uphill situation have a practice swing of this method first. If it doesn't seem possible, revert to the other method. Whichever you use, take enough club to allow for the extra height.

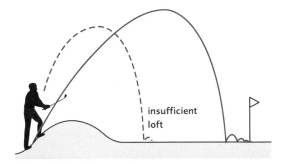

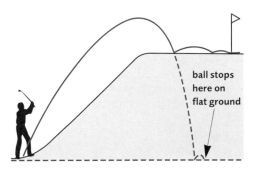

PITCHING UPHILL
When pitching from an upslope around the green, the ball will pop up high. The slope exaggerates the loft of the club. Don't use too lofted a club, or the ball will not run on forward sufficiently. When hitting uphill generally, take plenty of club to compensate for the extra height.

When pitching from an upslope near the green, remember the ball will travel higher than you probably imagine and won't go nearly far enough. The commonest error is to play a good shot but to leave the ball short. Use a narrow stance and allow yourself to follow through up the slope beyond impact. Don't use a sand wedge unless you want a particularly high, short shot. Use a pitching wedge or 9 iron to produce the trajectory and to keep the ball moving forwards.

When playing up a hill with a long shot, remember that the ball touches down before it has finished its full flight. Take plenty of club, mentally adding 10 or 20 metres (11 to 21 yards) to the length of your shot to cover the extra distance. But if you are landing on an elevated green high up above, remember that the ball touches down at a more horizontal angle. A ball landing on a green above you will always run and kick forwards. Expect the ball to finish at the back of the green. Don't over-compensate on your next round and under-club.

REMEMBER
USE A NARROW STANCE

...and in a Bunker!

Uphill and downhill lies can cause even more problems
in a bunker than they do on grass.

The most difficult bunker shot is a downhill
bunker shot from near the back of the
bunker. Again we have two problems. The
first is to make a good contact without
catching the sand behind the ball. The
second is that the downstroke takes off loft.

Address the ball with a very wide stance,
much wider than any other shot you ever
play. Keep the right foot straight in front, the
shoulders following the slope with the right
shoulder as high as possible. Allow the left
arm to bend slightly. Have two or three
rehearsals of the backswing, making sure that
you don't inadvertently scrape the sand
behind the ball. Keep your left shoulder low
and your right shoulder high and feel that
you really can get up and down the slope. If
you are a very accomplished golfer you
might be able to open the clubface slightly,
but be sure to keep the ball towards the toe
of the club in so doing. Leave a 5cm (2in)
gap between the club and the ball as with a
normal splash shot, and focus on taking sand
and the ball, following down and through
the sand beyond impact. At address the
clubshaft should point directly to you. Don't
allow the hands to creep forward or you lose
too much loft.

But the real problem with a downhill
bunker shot is that the ball will travel off far
lower than you expect. It is difficult to get a
ball up from a downhill lie and over a bank
in front of you. Think of going out sideways
if you have less height to negotiate or even
think of chipping out backwards. If you do
get the ball up and out over
the bunker, expect it to run.
For advanced golfers
playing this shot – and that
means four handicap or

better – try opening the clubface and almost
scooping the ball out with the right hand so
that the clubshaft flops onto your shoulder
at the end of the followthrough. Open the
clubface if you can, keeping the ball well
way from the neck of the club and up
towards the toe.

The standard uphill shot from under the
face of a bunker is easy. If you get right
under the face, approach the ball from
above, kneeling on your left knee and with
the right foot in the bunker. Remember
that you simply smash forwards into the
bottom of the ball and the upslope will
take it up.

A ball from a slight upslope in a bunker
can be awkward. As with other uphill lies
there is a choice of two methods. One way
of playing this shot is to use your pitching
wedge or sand wedge and simply to chip the
ball out, taking the ball and then the sand
beyond it. This requires a slow, firm swing
with a perfect contact of ball and then sand.
If you inadvertently catch the sand before
the ball, you are likely to lose length and the
ball may not pop out. But this is usually the
safest method for higher handicappers. The
other way of playing from a slight up-slope
is to play a splash shot, taking sand with the
ball. But on an upslope there is no sand
behind the ball, only air! To play a splash
shot, lean out at right angles to the slope,
shoulders following the slope. Address the
ball with a 5cm (2in) gap between the club
and the ball, focus on the sand and play as
normal a splash shot as you can, taking the
sand with the ball. You will find your
weight hangs back on your right foot. Good
contact with sand is crucial. The ball should
come out with good height.

REMEMBER
A DOWNSLOPE
TAKES OFF
HEIGHT

DIFFICULT SHOTS

Tricky bunker shots present probably the greatest challenge to the typical club golfer. As with any other aspect of golf, only practice makes perfect – combined with a positive attitude.

TRICKY LIES

On a downhill lie or from a hole in the bunker, the weight is kept exaggeratedly on the left foot, right shoulder very high. The club is then picked up steeply, even letting the left arm bend slightly, to produce a really steep downward attack.

Sloping Lies

Lies which involve you standing above or below the ball
on a side slope can be tricky to play.

When standing above the ball
you will automatically stand
closer to the ball and find
yourself bending over more.
The key to playing this shot well
is to maintain good balance. If
anything, you may find yourself
moving slightly down the slope
through impact, so take care to
address the ball in the middle of
the clubface or towards the toe.
Keep the ball centrally in your
own stance.

At the top of the backswing
the swing will be more upright
than normal. Just allow this to
happen and don't fight it.

Through impact it is crucial
to keep good balance and to stop
yourself from falling forwards.
Both heels will probably still be
on the ground through impact.
Look at the ball well to make
sure you strike it from the
middle of the clubface.

In keeping good balance
your foot work may be slightly
restricted. The followthrough
should naturally be high, with
the club coming up and over
your shoulder. In other words,

STANDING ABOVE THE BALL
When you play a shot from a sidehill lie standing
above the ball, it will tend to move left-to-right in
flight and then kick right on landing.

the whole swing should be on a much higher
and steeper plane than your normal swing.

The effect of this higher backswing and a
sloping lie is that the ball will invariably slice
away to the right. It will not only curve to the
right in the air but will also spin to the right on
landing. Remember that the ball will also
probably land on ground sloping the same way
and will therefore kick even further to the right

on landing. Most golfers fail to aim sufficiently
far left. With a 5 wood from such a lie, a top
woman golfer hitting the ball 160 metres (175
yards) or so might aim 45 to 55 metres (49 to
60 yards) left to allow for the slice and spin.

With an iron shot you may be able to
counteract the slope by turning the toe of the
club inwards at address and try to hold it
slightly closed through impact.

**STANDING BELOW
THE BALL**
Conversely, when you play
a shot from a sidehill lie
standing below the ball, it
will tend to move right-to-
left in flight and then kick
left on landing.

Sloping lies – below the ball

When standing below the ball your position
automatically puts you further away from it.
If you are small or the slope is steep and the
club feels alarmingly long, grip down it
slightly. If not, keep gripping at the end.

With this stance the swing should
automatically be much flatter, going around
your body. Remember that the plane of the
swing should follow the clubshaft at address.
In this case the swing will be flat and
rounded.

Through impact, balance is usually far
easier than when standing above the ball.
Stay firmly on both feet through impact
and watch the ball well. The clubface is
likely to close and the ball will invariably
turn to the left.

The followthrough again follows the whole
playing of the swing and will be much flatter
and more round the body. Don't fight it. Just
allow it to happen.

The flatter playing of swing and more
rounded attack will usually see the ball bend
away to the left. If you normally hook the
ball, this lie will exaggerate your fault. Aim
well away to the right and allow for the ball to
turn low and left.

Advanced golfers can counteract the slope
by holding the clubface slightly open at
address and through impact and keeping the
right hand further over in the grip.

With a short shot beside the green from
the same sloping lie, or with the ball on this
slope in a bunker, allow for the ball to turn
quite dramatically to the left.

Why Fade Your Driver?

Many golfers hit the ball reasonably straight with all their shots except
for those with a driver. Remember the principle that loft kills side spin.
The reduced loft of a driver will often produce a slice. The added loft of
a 5 wood will hit the ball much straighter. For most women, a driver of
12 degrees or more will minimize slicing.

The danger in using a driver is that the loft of
the club may look uninviting. If you aren't
careful, the tendency is to hold the clubface
up and open through impact, consciously or
sub-consciously trying to make loft. A club
with too little loft will exaggerate this
tendency.

To counteract slicing with a driver, tee the
ball up really high – as high as you dare
without the feeling of going underneath it –
and imagine the ball is on a side slope with a
ball above your feet. Refer to the previous
section for the technique.

Allow your weight to be a little more on
your heels than with an iron and treat the

shot as if it were a ball above your feet. With
a ball above your feet it should draw or hook
away to the left and not slice away to the
right.

If you hit the ball high and to the right
with a driver, the worst thing you can do
is to tee the ball lower. This encourages an
up-and-down, chopping action.

To get rid of the slice, remember that the
clubface must begin to look down to the grass
and not up to the sky through and beyond
impact. Make some practice swings, holding
the clubhead 25 or 30cm (10 or 12in) above
the ground and feel the roundness of the
swing and the clubface turning over.

TEE-UP CORRECTLY
Tee-up high with your
driver and get your
weight more onto your
heels than you would
do with an iron.

ADVANCED FADE WITH THE DRIVER

Top professionals (like Australian Karrie Webb, at Sunningdale, England) will not deliberately aim away from trouble but will instead fade or draw their shots to avoid obstacles and still end up in the optimum position on the fairway.

REMEMBER
TEE HIGH,
THINK SIDE
SLOPE

This is a section for advanced golfers who, having learnt to hit the ball straight, can then learn to bend the ball slightly from left to right or right to left. The benefit of this is that if you understand how to bend the ball it also teaches you how not to bend the ball if having problems.

Drawing a drive. Being able to bend a ball from right to left with a driver will give you added distance. The ball should touch down and then kick forwards. A drive with any slice spin will lack run. Refer to the previous section. To draw the ball, tee it up as high as you dare and create the feeling of roundness as though hitting the ball from a side slope. With a ball above your feet you would play it somewhere just ahead of centre in the stance and not right opposite your left heel. Use the same approach with this shot. Hold the clubhead off the ground at address, clubshaft pointing to your navel. Don't change the grip. The idea is to bend the ball no more than 5 metres from right to left in the air so don't over-compensate with the stance. As you move through impact, allow the clubface to turn over very slightly. At the end of the swing feel your arms squash onto each other with the elbows staying as close together as possible. The feeling should be of the left elbow being under the right one. The followthrough may feel slightly restricted without the wrist loosening. This should allow the clubface to start turning over through and beyond impact. If this should develop into a hook, make the same feeling of hitting from low to high, turning the arms over but with height to the finish. Think of hitting slightly up and over like topspin with a racquet.

Fading a drive. On a narrow fairway, particularly without of bounds down the left, the correct shot for a good player is often to start the ball down the left of the fairway with a little bend from left to right. This may lose length but is a controlled shot that won't run too far. Do just the opposite from drawing the

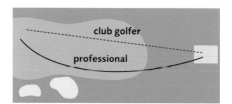

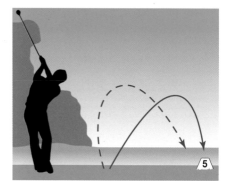

AVOIDING TROUBLE
With trouble down the left, the professional usually tries to aim towards it and fade the ball away from it. In contrast, the club golfer should turn to aim away from it (see diagrams above).

drive. Tee the ball down lower. Stand taller. Give yourself the illusion of standing on a slope slightly above the ball from which you would feel that the ball would bend away to the right. You need to ensure that the hands don't work too loosely or freely through impact. Put the right thumb straighter down the front of the club and press with it.

Through impact, keep the hips moving slightly early and quicker in relation to the hands and feel that the hands are a little slower and firmer. This should hold the clubface very slightly open and allow the ball to move 3 or 4 metres left to right. The key is the weight distribution and the feeling of standing above the ball.

Slicing round a tree. To create a big slice may require a change of grip. Keep your left hand well round to the left and the right hand well over. Open the clubface slightly at address and try to hold it open through impact. The key with this shot is to aim sufficiently far left. The ball may even start slightly right of your stance, so make sure you aim in the direction you intend to start the ball. The ball will also usually take up added height and lose length. The feeling of the swing should then be of swinging up and down, in an out-to-in direction, with quick hits and slow hands.

Hooking round a tree. To hook a ball round a tree, use a reasonably straight-faced club. Remember that loft kills side spin; if you take too much loft, you can't create the hook. Aim

well to the right of your obstacle. Put the right hand very well underneath the club. Have two or three practice swings and feel the clubface turn right over through impact so that it is face down in your followthrough. Start the ball out to the right of your obstacle. It will often start left of your stance. Turn the clubface over through impact with a flat, round the body followthrough.

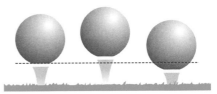

VARY YOUR TEE HEIGHT
Changing your tee height can help you draw and fade drives. More height helps keep the ball left, less height helps keep it right.

HOOKING AROUND A TREE
To hook around a tree or other trouble, aim your stance and swing right and the clubface left. Strengthen the grip and produce a flat, round-the-body action. It is generally easier to get a large hook on the ball than to slice.

SLICING AROUND A TREE
Slice around a tree by setting your stance and swing left, the clubface open and the right-hand grip tighter than normal. Watch out for extra height and keep away from the branches.

REMEMBER
FEEL THE
CLUBFACE

Playing the Course

Unlike most other sports, a game of golf involves playing not only your opponent but the golf course as well. Every course is different, offering a unique mix of obstacles to overcome. The key to good golf is to prepare yourself as well as you can for the challenges that lie ahead. For a club golfer, this might mean simply thinking about the best position from which to play the ball on each tee. For the professional, it can mean taking incredibly detailed and thorough notes of distances and positions of hazards in pre-tournament practice rounds. Either way, thinking about your strategy, general course management and the positive visualization of every single shot will all reap benefits. Anybody who simply steps up to the ball and hits it – without thought for where they want it to end up, the pitfalls they need to avoid and the suitability of their shot for that particular hole – will never make a good golfer. On the other hand, the prudent planner who thinks about her game will have a natural advantage every time.

Sophie Gustafson of Sweden playing in the Women's British Open at Woburn Abbey, England.

Strategy for Driving

Good driving is probably the most important part of the game. Women don't have as good powers of recovery as men do. We need to hit the ball onto the fairway every time.

1 Remember that you can choose exactly where on the tee you tee up your ball. Don't simply follow the players you are playing with. The view from one side of the tee can be completely different from the view from the other side. The general rule is to aim away from the trouble. If there are trees down the left side of the fairway, tee up on the left side. This will allow you to aim away from the trees as you aim towards the middle of the fairway. If there is trouble on the right, tee up on the right side of the tee and aim away from the trouble.

2 Remember that you can always go back up to two club lengths from the tee markers. Find a perfectly flat piece of ground. The teeing ground is the one place on the course where you can pick loose grass and tread down behind the ball. Get used to being selective with where you tee the ball and always tread down behind it to ensure you will make a smooth take-away. If you aren't satisfied with your position once you stand to the ball, start all over again. Be fussy.

3 Aiming left from the tee can cause problems. Ladies' tees in particular often don't aim where you want to hit the ball! In order to aim left, tee the ball up on the right side of the tee. Then have a practice swing to the right side of your ball. This will give you an exaggerated feeling of aiming to the left and swinging to the left. Then when you set up to the ball turning and aiming to the left should feel easier.

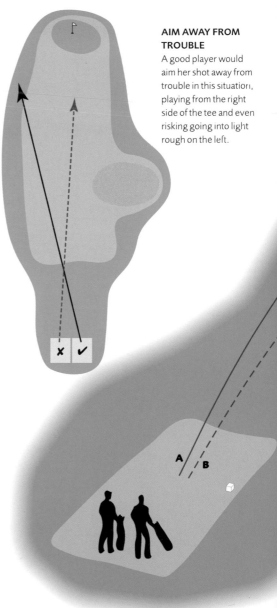

AIM AWAY FROM TROUBLE
A good player would aim her shot away from trouble in this situation, playing from the right side of the tee and even risking going into light rough on the left.

OPEN UP YOUR APPROACH SHOT
In this situation you should avoid the
bunker to the left and risk playing into
the light rough on the right, just to
open up the shot to the green.

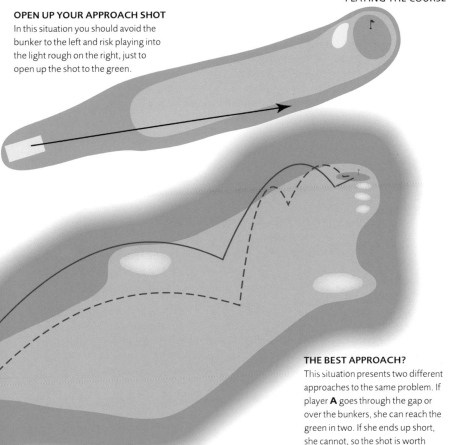

THE BEST APPROACH?
This situation presents two different
approaches to the same problem. If
player **A** goes through the gap or
over the bunkers, she can reach the
green in two. If she ends up short,
she cannot, so the shot is worth
trying. **B**'s more cautious route will
take three shots to the green.

➤ Plan the line and length of your target
carefully. Ideally choose a target not only on
the line you want to hit but roughly the
length you want. This will usually prove
more successful than choosing an object on
the horizon. If there is no target to aim at,
imagine a large white tablecloth spread out
on the fairway where you want the ball to
land. Never think of the obstacles you want
to avoid. Choose a very specific point to
aim to.
➤ Always aim away from trouble. If there is a
bunker at driving distance, don't just aim

five metres away from it. Be prepared to aim
20 metres away and allow yourself a greater
margin for error.
➤ When playing a long hole, or when an
opponent drives further than you do, never
try to hit the ball too hard. Concentrate on
good timing and hit the ball your normal
distance. If you press for length, your
direction tends to deteriorate.
Swing smoothly and just think
of making the loudest noise you
can on the back of the ball for
maximum distance.

REMEMBER
AIM AWAY
FROM
TROUBLE

Recovery Shots

The golden rule with all recovery shots is to get yourself safely back into play. Assess how much you can achieve with your recovery shot. If you are within striking distance of the green but realistically can't reach it, be content to take two shots. Play a sensible shot out on to the fairway and leave yourself in position for the next one.

From thick rough take a lofted club. Lofted clubs are also the heaviest. Think of using your 9 iron or pitching wedge. Use a reasonably wide stance, keep the shoulders as level as possible to give yourself an up and down swing. Feel that you pick the club up in the backswing and beat down through the ball. If the rough is very long it may grab the clubface and turn it to the left. If you are recovering from rough on the right side of the fairway, the danger is of careering across the fairway into the rough the other side. If playing from the left, the danger is of staying in the rough. Be realistic and beat it out.

Using a 5 wood or 7 wood from light rough can be much easier than using a long iron. The club is less likely to get twisted in your hand. But again, be realistic about how much you will achieve with a perfect shot. Remember, 'a wood in the rough means wood in your head!'.

Decide exactly where you are trying to finish with your recovery shot. If you are

A KEY PART OF THE GAME

Even top professionals can get into deep trouble on a regular basis. Here (right), Liselotte Neumann plays out of heavy rough. Recovery shots are an important part of the game for every player – no matter how good at golf you become, there will always be times when you have to make them. The important thing is to assess the shot realistically with a cool head, and then play it with the belief that you will make it.

playing out from the rough or from trees, walk onto the fairway and see where you would like the ball to be for your next shot. When hitting from trees it is easy either to under-hit and still leave yourself behind other trees or to over-hit and be in trouble on the other side of the fairway.

When playing from trees, use a punch shot (pp. 138–9). Have two or three practice swings and remember that your swing with the ball will always be longer than a practice swing. Keep well below the tree branches. Remember, a tree may be 90 percent air when you are watching someone else, but it is 90 percent wood when you do it yourself!

If you are in difficulty, remember the sensible option of picking out for two club lengths not nearer the hole. You can often achieve far more by taking this penalty stroke than by attempting to play the shot. You must drop the ball within two club lengths not nearer the hole but it can run up to another two club lengths, again not nearer the hole. Learn how to take a penalty drop. It can be useful.

REMEMBER

Try never to play two consecutive shots from the rough. Get yourself back on the fairway at all costs. On the golf course, trouble breeds more trouble unless you deal with the first recovery shot in a pragmatic fashion.

Be realistic about what you can achieve. Always listen to common sense and don't be greedy with the shots you try to make.

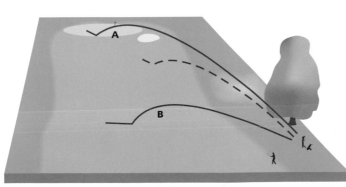

BE REALISTIC

Think about your route out of a difficult situation. If you are a good player, maybe you can make the green (**A**). If not, don't risk failure (the dotted line), but play the simple shot (**B**).

REMEMBER
DON'T BE
GREEDY!

Making the Right Decisions

Many club golfers play good shots but don't make sensible decisions. Very often they don't make a decision at all and hit the ball without a definite plan in mind. There are certain situations on the golf course that catch people time and time again.

On a dog leg hole (see pp. 176–7) the typical fault is trying to cut the corner. By cutting the corner you don't usually reduce the length of the shot into the green by as much as you imagine. You also risk going in the trees or rough and can leave a more difficult directional shot into the green. The golden rule with a dog leg is always to take the widest route round the dog leg. You may give yourself a slightly longer shot into the green but it will usually be easier and safer.

Many golfers always want to hit straight at the flag and never seem prepared to zig-zag. As soon as they see the flag they want to hit straight through trees, hedges, brick walls, rain shelters – anything but play safely. The higher your handicap and shorter your experience with golf, the more likely you are to make this error. Look at any obstacle you need to avoid and aim well away from it. Look at the shape of the green and the approach you would like. Be prepared to zig-zag to the left of the fairway if it leaves you a more open shot to the green. Don't just aim at the flag.

When playing to the green, learn to aim away from the flag. Greenkeepers like to tempt golfers into bunkers and ponds by putting a flag alarmingly close to them. You are unlikely to hit so close to the flag that your next putt is a certainty. Be prepared to aim away from the flag to the largest and safest part of the green. You will probably be just as close. It is often easier to get close to a flag by hitting five paces left of it than by trying to go straight towards it and misjudging the distance. If aiming away from the flag, try to picture another target where you want to land or look at something behind the green and fix your sights on that for direction.

With a cross bunker or pond in front of you,

USE YOUR HEAD
Think carefully about every shot before you play it, as Catrin Nilsmark is doing here in the Solheim Cup at Muirfield.

remember that you have five choices. You can go left of it, right of it, over it, short of it, or in it! Many golfers just don't make a decision at all. They get caught between all four sensible choices and finish up in the hazard.

With a cross bunker just in front of the green it may be worth attempting to carry it, even if a little risky, if you have a chance of landing on the green. If your bunker play is good, you may not be much worse off being in the bunker than just short of it. But if the bunker is 40 paces or more short of the green, your successful shot may not finish on the green anyway. If you land in the bunker you may not be able to recover onto the green. Weigh up the situation sensibly.

Are you just a gambler at heart who can't resist trying the carry, or are you really going to achieve something?

Learn to play for position. If there is a downhill area short of the green, think of playing short of it. If the shot from the left of the fairway into the green is much easier, then be prepared to be in light rough to the left rather than in the middle of the fairway. If playing short of a ditch or bunker, know your distance as accurately as possible. Most people playing short, play too short. Try to think of the mistakes the golf course designer and greenkeeper are trying to make you make, and don't make them!

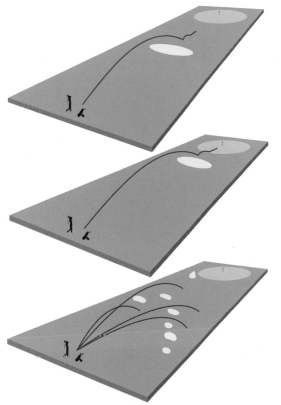

CROSS BUNKERS

When you face a cross bunker away from the green, assess your chances of success and failure. If you go in the bunker, can you play out onto the green?

BUNKERS NEAR GREENS

When attempting to carry a cross bunker near a green, take a risk – especially if your bunker play is good.

DIAGONAL CROSS BUNKERS

This kind of bunker in the fairway means that there will be a variety of routes you can take, depending on how good a player you are.

REMEMBER WIDEST ROUTE ROUND DOG LEGS!

Good scoring is a real art. It is often a question of making better decisions and understanding the thoughts of the golf course designer and greenkeeper as they try to trick you into trouble! The nine holes shown over the next few pages are designed to show you typical golfing situations and how to play them.

1 **Par five 485 yards dog leg.** The correct drive here is well left of centre to give you a clear shot around the corner. Tee up on the right side to help aim away from trouble on the right. The next shot is important. From the correct driving position you can turn between the two clumps of trees and have a straight forward third shot into the green. From the wrong driving position you may clip the trees on the corner of the dog leg or be forced towards the other clump of trees. You are likely to give yourself a more difficult shot to the green over the left-hand bunker.

2 **Par four 330 yards offset green.** Watch for this on a short par four. The correct drive is well down the right side, into light rough on the right if necessary. From here you have a clear shot at the flag along the length of the green. The drive in the centre of the fairway is not ideal. Here the second shot is more difficult. You are playing across a bunker and onto the narrow width of the green. Look at the flag position from the tee to work out the ideal drive. If you cannot see it, check the green if you pass it playing another hole.

3 **Par four 285 yards short dog leg.** If you are a long hitter you are tempted to reach the green. The large tree and ditch to the right make the drive at the green risky. You probably don't manage a brave enough line and probably can't carry the tree anyway. The correct drive is to keep short enough to have a straight line into the green. Hitting too far leaves a much more difficult second shot.

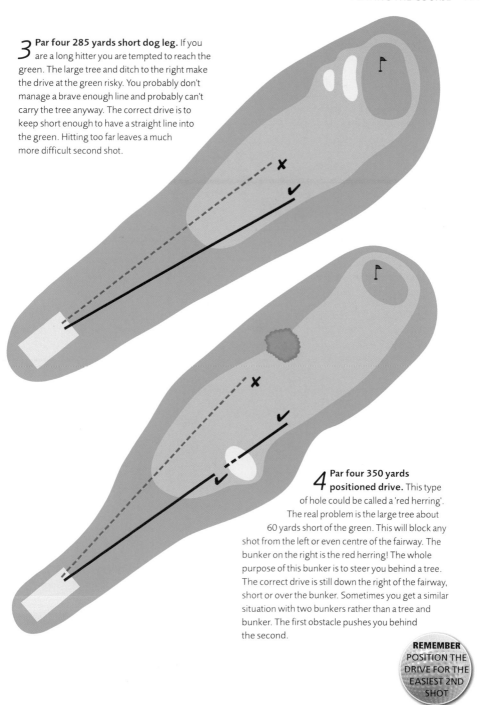

4 **Par four 350 yards positioned drive.** This type of hole could be called a 'red herring'. The real problem is the large tree about 60 yards short of the green. This will block any shot from the left or even centre of the fairway. The bunker on the right is the red herring! The whole purpose of this bunker is to steer you behind a tree. The correct drive is still down the right of the fairway, short or over the bunker. Sometimes you get a similar situation with two bunkers rather than a tree and bunker. The first obstacle pushes you behind the second.

REMEMBER
POSITION THE DRIVE FOR THE EASIEST 2ND SHOT

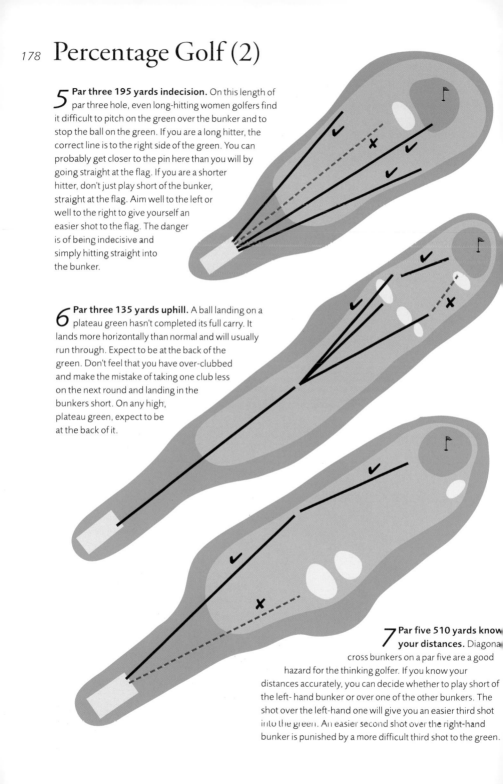

5 **Par three 195 yards indecision.** On this length of par three hole, even long-hitting women golfers find it difficult to pitch on the green over the bunker and to stop the ball on the green. If you are a long hitter, the correct line is to the right side of the green. You can probably get closer to the pin here than you will by going straight at the flag. If you are a shorter hitter, don't just play short of the bunker, straight at the flag. Aim well to the left or well to the right to give yourself an easier shot to the flag. The danger is of being indecisive and simply hitting straight into the bunker.

6 **Par three 135 yards uphill.** A ball landing on a plateau green hasn't completed its full carry. It lands more horizontally than normal and will usually run through. Expect to be at the back of the green. Don't feel that you have over-clubbed and make the mistake of taking one club less on the next round and landing in the bunkers short. On any high, plateau green, expect to be at the back of it.

7 **Par five 510 yards know your distances.** Diagonal cross bunkers on a par five are a good hazard for the thinking golfer. If you know your distances accurately, you can decide whether to play short of the left-hand bunker or over one of the other bunkers. The shot over the left-hand one will give you an easier third shot into the green. An easier second shot over the right-hand bunker is punished by a more difficult third shot to the green.

8 **Par four 340 yards The irresistible dare!** The bunkers or trees on the corner of this dog leg may be just too irresistible. There is a feeling of being able to carry the bunker. In reality you may not be able to carry it and in any event it possibly achieves nothing. Beware of a bunker like this with another hidden bunker or thick rough beyond it. If you do make the carry over the first hurdle, you will probably land in another danger area. The bunker by the green is there to make the second shot more difficult for those who can't resist the carry. Remember to take the widest route round the dog leg for an easier shot into the green.

9 **Par four 295 yards two tier green.** Watch for the short par four with a two tier plateau green, particularly if the green is small. A plateau often drains well and a ball pitching on it will not hold. If playing to the upper layer of a two tier green, aim to be able to run the ball up onto the top layer. The shortness of the hole may tempt you to hit wildly off the tee. Instead make certain the tee shot is accurate, giving yourself a clear run at the green without having to pitch over bunkers.

REMEMBER LOOK AT THE POSITION OF THE FLAG

Judging Distances

Judging distance well and taking the right club are essential to good scoring. Men tend to judge distance better; it is a psychologically proven phenomenon. It is noticeable on the golf course.

The first stage with your long game is to know how far you hit the ball with each club. Ideally for a reasonably long hitting woman golfer there should be a 9-metre (10-yard) gap in distance between adjacent irons. A good amateur golfer would probably hope to carry the ball 135 metres (150 yards) with a 5 iron, and then up or down 9 metres (10 yards) from there. Most are unlikely to have a 10-yard gap between the 3 and 4 iron, but the 7 wood and 5 wood take over from there. Learn to judge distances, either by pacing off the distances with well-hit shots, assessing where they land and not where they run, or use the par 3 holes on your home course for reference.

Club golfers invariably under-club. Be realistic. Firstly, remember that most trouble around greens is at the front. If you pitch to the flag you avoid most of the bunkers. Secondly, the distance from the front of the green to the flag is often foreshortened. But more important, if the flag is anywhere behind centre on the green it will probably look far nearer to the back of the green than it really is. You may think there is a space of 5 or 6 paces to the back of the green, with bushes or rough beyond. In reality the distance is usually much greater than we imagine. There are probably 20 paces between the flag and the trouble beyond the green. Get used to looking at the positions of flags on the green as you pass them when playing other holes.

Under-club by one club – 10 paces – and you risk three-putting. Convince yourself that there aren't man-eating tigers over the back of greens. The world is round, not flat, and there is just as much space beyond the flag as in front of it. When you watch players approach the

GO FOR THE FLAG
Don't be afraid to pitch or chip straight to the flag (as Kristal Parker is doing here). Too many club golfers under-club and leave their ball infuriatingly short, making the putts to follow more difficult.

green from the side it seems ridiculous that they are constantly short.

In order to improve, try to pass the flag on every single shot you play. Keep a note on your scorecard. Give yourself a point every time your shot to the green finishes on the green beyond the flag. Professionals find this scoring zone far more often than club golfers. Many club golfers soon discover that they never, ever pass the flag.

To judge distance well, do not select the club to be used until you are right at the ball – not even 10 metres before you get to it. Don't think ahead of yourself.

1 A flag towards the back of the green probably looks closer to the back than it really is and may tempt you to under-club. Look at other greens on your way round the course.

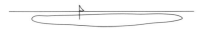

2 Flags are not always uniform height. A tall flag can look closer than it really is; a small one can make the shot look longer. Judge the distance to the green with people on it.

3 Large bunkers can look deceptively close.

4 Beware of undulations that appear just in front of the green. There may be 30 or 40 metres of hidden ground, tempting you to under-club.

5 Very flat ground can be difficult to judge, with hidden ground and distances you just don't see.

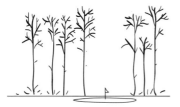

6 Tall trees can look closer than they really are or may make a flag look very small and further away than it actually is.

7 Try to judge distance with the people in front on the green. If there is hidden ground you can often learn about the distance by watching them walk to the green and counting the number of paces they take.

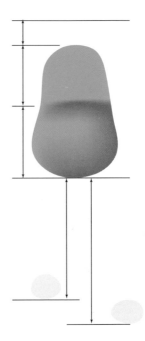

8 Professional golfers hardly ever play competitively without precise knowledge of distances. They carry notebooks and make copious notes in practice rounds for use in the tournament. An example of recording the distances of the hole above might look as shown in the following: Hole 5 – pine tree R fg 115 cg 128 bg 141 +25. This, in shorthand terms, means the pine tree right to the front of the green is 150 yards, to the centre of the green 128 yards, to the back of the green 141 yards, with 25 yards over the back of the green before any trouble.

REMEMBER ALWAYS AIM TO PASS THE FLAG

Bad Weather Blues

When the wind is blowing or you are being soaked by the rain, everyone on the course is suffering the same problem. Don't be downhearted. Just think of it as another golfing challenge.

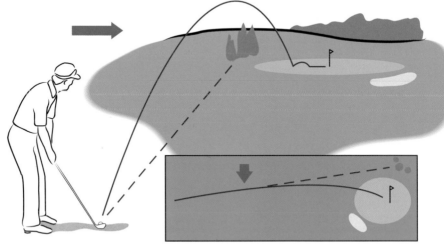

ALLOWING FOR WIND
Allow for a side wind by aiming to a new target to the side of the green. Aim the clubface, stance and swing at this target and let the wind do the rest.

Suitable kit is vital in the wet. Make sure you carry an umbrella, preferably a bright one to cheer you up. Keep a towel hanging inside it. If you wear glasses, fit a visor to them. Wear waterproofs that are comfortable and don't impede your swing. Always have at least one spare glove in your golf bag, preferably in a polythene bag. And finally, the best things for keeping your hands dry are mittens over your golf glove. In windy conditions, wear clothing that doesn't flap about and distract you.

Here are some useful hints for playing in the rain:
➤ Keep a dry ball for driving. A wet ball dives rather than flies.
➤ If it is extremely wet, take your practice swings before teeing up the ball to keep it as dry as possible.

➤ Keep the handles of your clubs dry and in the bag as long as possible, with a hood over it for protection.
➤ While waiting for your partners to drive off, keep your club dry and return it to the bag as soon as possible after use.
➤ The rain can make recovery shots from the rough difficult. Don't be greedy, but get back on the fairway at all costs.
➤ Wet greens initially become slippery and the ball skids. As they get wetter, they quickly lose this slipperiness and become slower.

Playing in the wind
In windy conditions, always toss some grass up to check which way the wind is blowing before you play the shot. Don't wait until you have played the shot and then think of the wind!

DIRECTION

Look at the flag to judge the direction of the wind and, in particular, be wary of a sheltered tee and exposed fairway or green – and vice versa. You may stand on a tee and not feel the wind. But once the ball leaves the trees, it gets blown off line. Sometimes you may allow for the wind and forget that the green is sheltered. Always look at the flag or flags on nearby greens.

Swing smoothly and keep perfect balance. Exaggerate this by holding your balance for at least four or five seconds. In windy conditions, the danger is of your swing being blown inside out!

SIDE WIND

With a side wind, allow for it and don't fight it. Aim your stance, clubface and swing to a new target and let the wind do the rest. If you are a low handicap player, you can try to bend the ball into the wind to hold it straight. Open or close the clubface at address, depending on the direction of the wind.

HEAD WIND

Think of a head wind as adding up to four clubs to the shot and take plenty of club. 'Pros' will usually think in terms of a 1, 2, 3 or 4 club wind or mentally add 10 to 40 metres to the shot before choosing a club to use. The more accurate your knowledge of distances, the better. Swing slowly and don't fight the wind. You are unlikely to hit through the back of the green, so attack the flag.

When driving, offset the effect of the wind with a lower trajectory. Tee the ball a little lower or, better still, aim to leave the tee in the ground. Experienced players may aim for a slightly flatter swing plane and use a stiffer-wristed action to reduce the backswing. Good balance is vital. Remember that an off-line shot tends to be exaggerated, with the ball rising and spinning more quickly.

DOWN WIND

Here it is important to drive the ball high enough. Tee it up to get good height, make sure you get the peg out of the ground as you hit and, if necessary, use a 3 wood to achieve enough elevation. This may send the ball farther than a driver. A wind from behind tends to flatten the shot and keep the ball down; it also tends to straighten out bending shots.

When playing onto the green, take off up to four

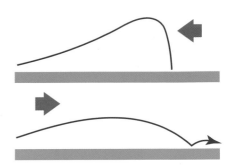

DIFFERENT WINDS

Head winds make the ball fly higher and take it off line (above, top). Down winds make the ball fly lower and if anything help straighten out the shot (above, bottom).

PUTTING IN WIND

Windy conditions will also affect the way the ball rolls on the green. If it is very windy, don't ground the club and keep it well away from the ball in case it moves.

clubs and remember that the ball bounces on landing. So a softer ball may stop better. *REMEMBER* If you do go through the green, your pitch shot back is into the wind. Over-club through the green and the chances are you will then under-hit when coming back. This is one of the classic ways for a good player to drop a shot without seeming to do much wrong.

Very windy conditions can affect the ball on the green just as much as they do the long game. This is particularly the case on a fast green when playing downwind.

REMEMBER
EXTRA GOOD
BALANCE
IN HIGH
WINDS

When you approach any golf shot, it is important to have a positive picture of the shot you are trying to play. You should stand on the tee and visualize the ball flying through the air to your target. This picture of the shot you are trying to produce acts as the set of instructions to your brain and body, telling you what to do.

Unfortunately, what easily happens is that instead of picturing the shot you want to produce, you picture the shot you are trying to avoid. It is no good thinking to yourself, 'please don't let me go in that bunker' and having a vivid picture of the bunker. Nor is it any good thinking 'please don't let me go out of bounds like I did here yesterday'. If you have a vivid picture of the ball slicing out of bounds, then that too acts as the instructions to your brain and body and will almost certainly produce a slice.

The same can apply to longer handicaps. If you stand behind a pond and hope that

you don't go in it, the picture in your head is probably of the ball dribbling into the water. Your body responds and does just that. Similarly, if you imagine missing a putt to the left, you will probably miss it to the left. Positive thinking really means giving yourself a set of positive instructions.

It is vital for every shot you play that you choose a target. Most golfers imagine they do this. Very few actually do. Most players look down the fairway and try to avoid trouble. Their idea is of trying to aim left of a bunker or right of trees. Their idea of choosing a target is

SEE THE SHOT
Concentrate on your tee shot ending up in the perfect position – don't allow negative thoughts of failure before you hit the shot.

THINK IN THE PRESENT
Eliminate memories of past mistakes. Think about the shot and the round you are playing today, not yesterday or tomorrow.

usually simply avoiding obstacles – perhaps driving between trees. This means that the picture in their head is not of the place they are aiming for but of the trouble they want to avoid. If you picture the trees, you will be drawn there like a magnet. The correct way of choosing a target is to pick out some point on the horizon or, even better, at the distance you hope to hit, and focus on that.

When driving down the fairway, choose where you want to land and from your imagination take out a large, white tablecloth. Lay it out there in the middle of the fairway and picture your drive landing or running neatly onto it.

When we address the ball the target we are aiming at is invisible. You need a clear picture of it out there to the left side of your head. If you don't have a clear picture of the target there is a tendency to look up too soon, trying to see the ball and the target at the same time. If you can't picture the flag or other target, you might as well be hitting off the side of a ship on a dark, foggy night. Know where the target is. Picture it in the left side of your head.

Whether you are standing on the tee waiting to play or simply have a spare moment at home, picture playing shots in your imagination. Simply rehearsing shots at home or before you play can make it easier to have positive thoughts on the course, which will more often than not translate into better golf shots. For example, if there is a par 3 that you don't like or haven't played well in the past, imagine yourself hitting perfect shots to it, over and over. This mental practice should help you make a positive picture of good shots when faced with the real situation in play. A good mental attitude for playing golf is all about banishing negative thoughts and bad pictures from the mind.

THINK SUCCESS
Imagine your approach shot rolling across the green and into the hole. In your mind's eye, visualize your putt ending up in the hole.

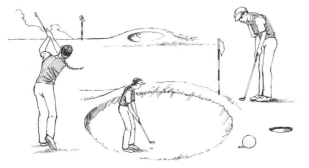

CONCENTRATE
Shut out of your mind the problems that face you and concentrate exclusively on the shot in hand.

REMEMBER
THINK
POSITIVELY:
PICTURE EVERY
SHOT

Practice and Winning

Your first two or three golf lessons can be the most important and start you well or badly. Always use a fully qualified professional and insist on taking a course of lessons – at least six and preferably ten. This gives your professional a chance to work systematically through the basic golfing techniques. Lessons must be followed by practice. Aim for at least 250 balls' practice between lessons and don't expect to see any dramatic improvement without a combination of lessons and practice. Don't be tempted to ask for too much information at each lesson. Good professionals will give you one or two key points to work on and perfect. Be patient. Work methodically at each point in turn. It is all too easy to make the swing too complicated. Keep the swing simple: the rest of the game is hard enough!

When experimenting with your golf swing, only change one variable at a time. If you try to change more than one, you won't know what is having the effect.

Samantha Head of England the other half of the European Tour's twins.

Practice Makes Perfect

Keep a written note of what you learn and are working on. Remember that the same faults tend to creep in over and over again. Even experienced players often find basic problems arising with the grip or stance, for example, which recur right through their careers.

If possible, have your lessons videoed. The ideal method is for the professional to video you and comment audibly to give you a full record to study at home. Keep videos for future reference.

Make sure you have sessions on chipping, putting, pitching and bunker shots. Players often ignore the short game, but this is where scoring can improve most quickly. Depending on your standard, anything from 40 to 70 percent of your shots will be played from within 50 metres of the green. Spend the same percentage of time on lessons and practice with the short game.

Try, too, to have the occasional playing lesson. Your professional can then see you in action on the course and work on strategy, aiming and general course management. Often players who aim well on the practice ground do something quite different on the course. So give your professional an opportunity to see this.

Once you are an established player, have lessons when you are playing well. This gives the professional something to compare you with when things go wrong. It makes it easier to pick out problems and help correct them. Don't just go to the professional when you are desperate about your game and expect her to work miracles. Improving the swing can often mean producing worse shots before things get better. And results in terms of better scoring will take quite a few weeks of combined practice and play.

Women are often far better learning in group lessons. This is particularly the case when you start. Seeing other people making the same errors can be encouraging. You also have players with whom to play and practise

and swap ideas on progress. It is also much easier to learn without the pressure of a 'pro' standing over you for the entire 30 or 60 minutes.

Stay with one professional, but bear in mind this word of warning: the professional who makes the swing seem complicated may not be giving you a swing that will work on the course. Good lessons should make the swing seem progressively easier. Remember that an 8-year-old child can do it!

Long game practice

When practising your long game, always aim to a target, preferably a large one you might hit, such as an open umbrella. You will then have a reasonable chance of success and this will, in turn, boost your confidence. If you simply practise to a flag, the inevitable failure is discouraging and doesn't hold your attention. Set your target at the correct distance for each club and concentrate on every shot, trying to hit it to the best of your ability. Don't be careless.

Initially you will be working to improve your best shots. Good players then have to work at improving, then eliminating, bad shots. Always make an effort in practice to hit each shot well and try as hard as you would on the course.

WORK AT YOUR GAME
As is the case with all sports, if you want to become proficient at golf there is no substitute for hard work and regular practice. Nearly all top professionals work on their game all the time, and it is often those players who practise longest and hardest who are the most consistently successful.

REMEMBER
LEARN WITH
VIDEO

The Value of Routine

Golf is a stationary ball game. It can allow you too much time for thinking. The better your routine for approaching shots, the better your game will stand up to pressure.

There are three stages to playing good golf. The first is to be able to play the shots in practice and on the practice ground. The second is to take this method into play. The third is to be able to cope with pressure. A good routine gives you the security to cope with any situation.

Work at a routine in which you repeat the way in which you prepare for a shot. This encourages repetition in the golf swing itself.

Lining up

As an example of routine, get used to leaving your bag and clubs in the same position to the right of the ball. Line up in the same way in practice and in play. Either walk up to the ball from the side or, preferably, go around behind the ball and line up from there,

possibly over a spot in front of the ball. Do the same thing over and over again.

Preparation

Set your posture in the same way each time, with your hands going on the club in the same manner – first the left, then the right and so on. Learn not to fiddle with your hands but get your grip on the club in two movements. Once you are addressing the ball, become repetitive with the number of waggles or twirls of the club you do.

The finish

Learn to watch the ball well through impact and finish each swing with a perfectly balanced followthrough, holding it for a

good four seconds. Golf isn't like a moving ball game. You don't have to run after the ball! All you have to do is stand and admire it – or watch carefully to see where on earth it has gone! Even when you let the arms down, keep the legs balanced until the ball stops rolling. Watch the ball to the end of its flight and roll, without losing balance and walking away from it. Learn to repeat the swing and the whole routine from the moment you walk up to the ball to the time when you have finished the swing through.

Short game routine

Routine certainly does not stop when you get on to the short game. Use a definite routine when putting, as well. Read the green in the same way each time, have the same number of practice swings, keep your head still and aim for a repetitive stroke on every putting shot. When you are suddenly faced with an important putt, don't feel that you need to do two or three extra practice swings. It achieves nothing. Do the same as you would normally, however important the putt, and you have every chance of repeating your successful action.

Two-speed thinking

Learn, too, to look up the same number of times. Typically on the practice ground you pull a ball forward and then look up once at the target before hitting it. On the golf course you may do something quite different, perhaps looking up several times before the shot. In a competitive situation, you possibly look up even more, move your feet or shuffle out of position, allowing time for indecision. If you watch good golfers, you will see that they do virtually the same each time they play the ball. Emulate good golfers.

The brain makes decisions in two ways. In one way we make quick decisions, weighing up the situation at speed. We use this thinking in emergencies and in moving ball games. It is generally accurate and reliable. In the slower way of thinking we make judgements and choices in a very different way. It is more deliberate, using a completely different part of the brain. In golf, the danger is of using the quick speed thinking in practice or general play – look up once, twice and hit it. And then under pressure trying too hard and moving to the other style of thinking. The brain functions differently and judgement may be far worse. If you look up once to gauge your distance with a pitch shot when it seems easy, only look up once under pressure.

PRE-SHOT ROUTINE

Top-class players follow an exact pre-shot routine. You can almost set a stop-watch on them. Do the same. Go through the same rituals with each stage of your grip, stance, address and swing with every shot you play.

REMEMBER
DON'T SLOW DOWN UNDER PRESSURE

Relaxation, Concentration and Trying Too Hard

Golf is not a game where most people do their best when they try their hardest. Some players imagine they would hole a putt for a million dollars, others if it were to win the British Open. In reality, golf is a game which most people play best when feeling as relaxed as possible.

Tension in the shoulders, arms and hands is usually detrimental to performance. If you feel tension on the golf course, learn to breathe properly. Breathe out a few times.

For most golfers it is better to tackle the most important of events by thinking of them as 'just another round'. A friendly round with a few pals is the situation best suiting most people's games. The reason is that there is someone to relax with, someone to talk to. You tend to hit the ball, forget it, and carry on a conversation. You get to the next ball, switch off from the conversation and onto the shot. It tends to stop you from thinking from one shot to the next and making judgements too soon.

But in a competition situation it is easy for the game to be played in silence. Each player wants to do her best. Perhaps you are faced with someone you have never met before. You find her intimidating. She probably finds you intimidating. After the round you sincerely hope you never meet her or play with her again. And yet, in reality, there is nothing wrong with either of you! With no conversation you both start thinking forwards, worrying about the shot ahead, thinking of the past errors and trying too hard to make a score. The game gets slower and slower. The good shots are stifled by trying too hard. And the usual comment after the round is that you couldn't concentrate.

There are two ways of concentrating on the course. The first is to wrap yourself in a cocoon of concentration on the first tee, trying not to let any extraneous thoughts permeate the outer shell. The second way is to learn to switch on to the shot and to switch off between shots. This is how most golfers play their best. Trying to concentrate too hard tends to create tension.

The key is to be able to relax and then pinpoint concentration when you arrive at the ball. To relax, if you find this difficult, imagine that tension is a liquid inside the body. Take a few deep breaths and hang the arms down. Imagine the tension, a warm pink fluid, literally dripping into little pools beneath your hands.

To focus your attention and cast aside any unwanted thoughts of the previous conversation, make a statement to yourself. 'Hello ball. Here I am, 150 metres from the target. That is a 4 iron. I want to hit it to the best of my ability.' Switch on, focus on the ball and the target. Hit it, forget it, walk. Most players find it harder to switch off after the shot than to switch on before it. If you have to play in silence with a playing partner you don't know, learn to cope with it. Switch on, switch off. Letting your mind wander is far less tiring than focusing on the ball from start to finish.

Never think of the shot facing you until you reach the ball. Don't predict what club you need until you are right there – not even 10 metres before. The shot can look very different when you reach it. Don't waste effort thinking about it too soon.

See the game as being made up of a number of separate shots. Just play each to the best of your ability. Don't aim for making a

score but just let it happen. A real key is to assess your motivation for shots. Champions want to do their best shot every time; club golfers often have a fluctuating level of trying. One shot seems unimportant, another very important. Perhaps they are being watched. Maybe it is a shot over water. Perhaps they are scoring very well. Pressure mounts.

The correct way to approach the game is to think rationally: 'I want to do the shot to the best of my ability.' This is a far less pressurized way of approaching the game. Each should be approached methodically.

An ideal way of seeing the correct mental approach is playing a Texas Scramble. In this you all, of course, drive, but then you take the best drive, you all hit from that point, and so on. What this does is to teach players not to link shot to shot. There is an element of surprise. It is usually easier to forget one shot and then not think of the next until the choice is made. You learn to separate the shots mentally, seeing one shot at a time.

Develop a golfing method that will stand up under pressure. Many golfers do one thing on the practice ground, then change their technique on the course and finally change it

GETTING RELAXED
If you find it difficult to relax on the golf course, try muscle-relaxing exercises like rolling your head (above) or positive visualizations of tension release.

again when it really matters. The likely change now usually involves unnecessary slowing down and trying too hard. Instead of hitting every shot to the best or her ability and leaving it at that, the player probably tries to force the shot. Now she sees the shot as vital, has a couple of practice swings, hitches up the glove, fiddles with the clubhead, isn't satisfied with its cleanliness. She then moves behind the ball to choose a spot and can't seem to find one. Eventually, the decision having been made, she moves round to address. She then looks up once, twice, three times. Each has a more pained and worried expression than the one before. Eventually, after much pondering and far more shuffling than normal, she seems ready to make a strike. There is silence and stillness. The tension is all too apparent... she then decides that her trolley is in the wrong position and starts all over again!

REMEMBER
TRYING TOO
HARD IS
DESTRUCTIVE

Fear of Failure

Golf is a game more punishing than most. In most ball games you can get hurt – a broken nose, ripped off ears, twisted limbs. In golf, all you risk is a shattered ego...

To many people a shattered ego is far more punishing than physical dangers. Many top-class games players, confidently risking life and limb every time they walk on a pitch, are far more frightened of golf and the golf ball. We can make such asses of ourselves. It doesn't matter how great a golfer you are, stupid little errors are round the corner. The short missed putt, the fluffed pitch, and the bunker shot catching the face in front. For this reason, you rarely if ever find a conceited golfer – except amongst those inexperienced and naive at the nastiness of the game!

In order to play well, it is essential to remove all fear from yourself. In truth, the worst disaster you can face on the golf course is to lose a ball. It costs you money. But in reality you usually find another anyway. And yet many golfers are terrified of making a fool of themselves. The novice seems to think there are eyes staring out of every bush, other golfers always there, chuckling at their errors.

DIFFICULT SHOTS
Believe in yourself when you are faced with a difficult shot – perhaps out of an especially unforgiving bunker, for example. It is just another shot, and no one will laugh at you if you make a mess of it. Brandie Burton, left, in action at Muirfield.

VISUALIZE POSITIVELY
Tell yourself you can make the shot. Imagine you are your favourite 'pro' golfer and think how they would feel as they played the shot. Self-confidence is all in the game of golf, as Kellie Kuehne (right) shows in the US Women's Open.

In reality, the experienced golfer always turns away and pretends she hasn't seen, only too thankful that the error wasn't hers.

The average golfer is usually far too concerned over the score. Many are frightened of the card and pencil from the first tee. One bad hole brings out thoughts of a bad score. What will everyone say? Worries over the final total bring out the worst in her game. Her mind races ahead, irrationally thinking of the embarrassment facing her. The end of the round will be reached. The marker will want to check the score, calling it out hole by hole and bringing it all back. And then the card will be handed over. A signature required as if to acknowledge all the errors. 'Yes, it was me. I did it. I confess.' From there the wretched score is posted on the board for all to see. You imagine everyone homes in on your bad score and thinks the worse of you,

but they don't. Certainly not those who understand the game. And perhaps it will make the newspaper. They will all know.

You have to learn to play the game without fear of failing. You have to ooze confidence, with just the right degree of humility.

Consider your own feelings on the course. Rate your confidence, or lack of it, on a scale from 1 to 9. At the lower end – 1 – is a feeling of 'I feel absolutely terrified and wish I wasn't here'. We then work through feelings of being terrified, worried, apprehensive, calm, reasonably confident, positive, very confident, aggressively positive and confident. To many, the feelings are always hovering around 3 and 4. The good golfer, in any situation, needs to feel around 8 and 9 – whether she is on the first tee, the 18th green, playing a putt to save the match, or playing a putt to win. The aspiring champion needs ➤

REMEMBER
BELIEVE IN
YOURSELF!

➤ to feel like a winner and walk like a winner. To those on an adjoining fairway she should portray cool confidence and look as though she is both enjoying the game and succeeding. If faced with a daunting shot, ask yourself how Alison Nicholas would feel. 'I am Alison Nicholas. I will hit the ball like Alison Nicholas.' She isn't going to be worried about losing a new ball.

On the first tee, feel in command in the match even before you tee off. Don't trudge onto the tee, nervously and apologetically with suggestions that you are overawed and honoured to play with your opponent (unless she really is a superstar). Don't utter some drivel about hoping you give her a game. Be confident. 'Hi I'm Sally. Have a good game. I'm playing a Titleist 2.' Establish who's boss from the start. Look organized and determined.

Learn to play badly – and enjoy it!
Anyone can cope with playing well; the art is to learn to cope with playing badly. If you can still survive and enjoy the game after an horrendous day, you suddenly find they aren't so likely to happen. If you panic, then bad turns to worse. Obviously, to be a champion you have to have self pride. You want to do your best. You can't be complacent. But fear of bad scores is, in the main, what causes them. So, how do we cope with a bad round?

One player will come in full of smiles. To shouts of how had she done, her first comment is that it was awful, truly awful – a

disaster. Then someone will ask: 'But what was the score?'

'I'm not telling you. It was dreadful, but I enjoyed it. I saw parts of the course I have never seen before – but my husband probably has! I had so much bunker practice my bunker shots reel rejuvenated and really I feel I've got rid of all the bad shots for the year, today. So watch out next month. My score? 94... no not 94 gross, 94 nett. But it was fun.'

Then, when others ask after your score, you find your friends becoming protective (thankful, of course, that it wasn't them): 'She didn't have a good day, but she enjoyed it.'

They are all so kind, sympathetic – at least any you can call true golfers, with their own ghastly experiences behind them. It wasn't so bad after all. They all come out with their own horror stories of bad rounds, missed putts and the 94 pales into insignificance. They are all so thankful they can go home and tell their husband and children there was someone worse than them. You are everyone's friend. A bad round need never hold any fears ever again.

But then there is the other character. She finishes her round, refuses to check the score accurately, scowls at her playing partner, 'I'd rather tear it up, but put it in if you must', thrusting the scorecard into her hand. She then storms to the car park, prizes open the boot of the car, flings in the clubs, trolley and all still attached, lurches into the driver's seat, still clad in golf shoes and drives out with a screech of burning rubber. All eyes turn from the clubhouse window. After mumbling and mutterings everyone knows

PLAYING OVER WATER
Many club golfers are intimidated by the thought of having to play over water – but then that is what it is there for: to put you off! If you play the shot as if it was any other, there is no reason why you should not make it. Liselotte Neumann shows how it is done at Les Bordes, France.

her score. Blow by blow is recounted by the playing partner, exaggerating her every disaster amidst squeals of delighted laughter.

And when the poor lady does pluck up courage to attack the course again, her entry into every part of the clubhouse is met with a deathly, embarrassed silence and knowing looks. Her next round gets worse – and the one after that even worse, remembering the pain from the past experience. If you can't cope with a bad score, they will happen. The pressure for many women is having to tell their husband and children (who may be better golfers then they are) how they played and scored! If that is the pressure, recite one of two simple facts – you did win, or you didn't win. Bore them with recounting your good shots – until they stop asking. If you win a raffle prize, simply say you won it at golf! Talk positively!

Golf is a game where there are no excuses. Try not to make any – the bad back, the noisy greenkeeper, the badly cut hole, the preparation for your daughter's wedding in September! Golf, you see, is the only game where you have your own ball. No one else touches it or influences it. You tee it up, you hit it, you pick it out of the hole, clean it, drop it. Everything that happens to it is your fault and your responsibility. It doesn't matter how well you learn to play, disaster can lurk just round the corner. The trick is to overcome each obstacle and accept that it is a game made up of missed shots. You can wait a lifetime for a hole in one. Every other shot is a miss! Any fool can hit good shots. Real improvement comes from learning to make the bad shots better.

Learn to make a stylish swing and walk like a champion. Players on an adjoining fairway probably won't see the flight of your ball. They will see your swing and your reaction to the shot. Look like a good player having a bad shot rather than a bad player having a bad shot!

REMEMBER
THERE ARE NO EXCUSES!

Strokeplay

Strokeplay – or medal play, as it is otherwise known – is generally considered to be the most testing form of competition in golf.

In strokeplay the total number of shots for the complete 18 holes is recorded. The scores for each hole are written down and added up to give the gross score.

The gross score is always used in professional competitions and championships. In amateur competitions, other than championships, the player's handicap is deducted to give the nett score. The lowest gross score wins the scratch prize and the lowest nett score the handicap prize.

In strokeplay, you are playing against a whole field of players rather than one specific opponent. For this reason, the rules and penalties for matchplay and strokeplay differ. In strokeplay your playing partner is correctly known as the marker. Before starting the round, players exchange scorecards and mark each other's cards throughout.

The strokeplay format is the one used for assessing handicap. It can be played as a singles, foursomes or fourball.

Many players are terrified of playing a medal card. The scorecard seems to put pressure on them. Every shot counts. In matchplay and other forms of competition a bad shot does not have such a punishing effect from a scoring point of view. Being a good strokeplay player requires a real understanding of the psychology of the game.

The first rule is keep firmly in the present. Think of the shot facing you now. Don't look forward and don't look backwards. The secret of playing a good medal round is to stand on the first tee and to hit the ball to the best of your ability. Walk to the next shot and hit it to the best of your ability. Don't try hard with one shot and relax with another. Simply hit it, forget and walk – one boring shot after another.

Eventually the ball arrives in the hole on the 18th green. Add up the score.

The danger is that most players are constantly looking backwards or looking forwards instead of thinking of the shot facing them NOW. Typically they start with a 10 on the first hole. They can't cast it from their mind. The 2nd, the 3rd the 4th are all ruined by thinking of the 10 on the first. How am I going to make up for it? You can't. It has gone, it's past, forgotten. Nothing will make some players forget the ten on the first... until they take 11 on the 9th!

Otherwise, they look back before playing the shot, remembering what they did in that situation the day before, week before, year before. They worry about the past. Don't look backwards. Most people don't learn from past mistakes. They simply condition themselves to make the same mistake again. Live firmly in the present.

Don't do what most players do and add up the score after nine holes, assuming that your score for eighteen holes will be double your first nine. Very few players ever record the same score for front nine and back nine! Don't try to predict the score. If doing well, don't start thinking of the prizes. Many a competition is lost by the player being distracted into assuming she has won.

Remember, too, that common sense sits right there on your left shoulder, whispering in your ear and telling you what to do. (For this reason, all good golfers keep the left shoulder up, just listening to common sense!) Don't ignore common sense if you feel you are doing very well or very badly. Don't become over-ambitious or over-cautious. Play your normal shot regardless of the score and wait and see what happens. A bad start doesn't mean a bad finish.

GOOD STROKEPLAY
Play each shot as it comes and eventually the ball will drop into the hole at the 18th. Only then may you celebrate if you have won! Here Sherri Steinhauer is victorious at Muirfield.

Dos and don'ts of strokeplay

➤ Don't become big-headed if things are going well.
➤ Don't think: 'What if?' – it signifies stress.
➤ Don't anticipate the score before the last shot is played.
➤ Do remember that a bad start does not mean a bad round.
➤ Put the score out of your mind until the match is over. If you are doing well, you may get over-excited; if you are doing badly, it can worry you and make things worse.
➤ Don't assume your final score will be double that of the first nine holes. A score can be made up of 45 out and 35 in or 35 out and 45 in. Keep going.
➤ Don't think about what you are going to win until you've won it.
➤ Don't worry about making the winner's speech until you know you've won the competition!

➤ The only form of forward thinking you should do is to plan each hole as you get to it.
➤ See where the flag is and plan your drive carefully.
➤ Don't predict your score. You must think firmly in the present.
➤ Hit the shot and then forget it. Walk to the ball and just concentrate on the next shot, then the next... and so on.
➤ Always play one shot at a time in your mind.
➤ Don't choose the club until you get to the shot or you will muddle your thinking.
➤ Think of each shot for itself. Don't remind yourself of shots past or anticipate shots to come.
➤ If you make a mistake, put it out of your mind as quickly as possible.
➤ Don't adjust your play for any hole because of the score. Use your normal approach to any one shot, regardless of where you stand in the match.
➤ Don't take unnecessary risks, particularly with recovery shots or those that contain elements of a gamble. If you feel things are going badly, you may make them worse.

To repeat: one of the biggest failures is indecision and doubt. Never, ever let yourself think 'What if?'. What if equals stress. 'What if I go in the bunker?' 'What if I go in the trees?' 'What if I don't win this competition?' If you go home not having won it you are in just the same position as you were when you arrived!

REMEMBER
THINK FIRMLY IN THE PRESENT

Matchplay

This is the form of competition in which you compete hole by hole against one individual or a partnership.

Matchplay is different from strokeplay, in which you are competing against the whole field of players on the score overall. In matchplay, the player with the lower score on each hole wins that hole, playing either level or off handicap.

Assume, for example, that golfer A is playing a match against golfer B and they are playing level. A wins the first hole with a four to B's five. A goes one up and correctly B should state the score – that she is one down. On the second hole, both players have five and they therefore halve the hole and A remains one up. A wins the third and goes two up, while B then is two down.

Say A is eventually three up after 15 holes – that is, three up with three to play. We now say that she is 'dormie three', meaning that she cannot lose unless they go into extra holes. A and B halve the 16th, so that A remains three up with only two holes left. At this point B cannot catch her and so we say that A has won by three holes up and two holes to play, abbreviated to 3 and 2.

If, for example, B won the 16th, 17th and 18th, the players would finish the match all square. It would depend on the rules of the competition and the format as to whether they went on to play extra holes. That would mean going down the 1st again, which then becomes the 19th. Or the match ends there.

If it is a knockout competition, then they would go on to the 19th, 20th and so on, until there was a definite winner. If it is a club or international match, then often the play would finish at the 18th and a halved match would be recorded.

Here are some points on golf etiquette:
➤ On the first tee you should toss for who gets the honour of

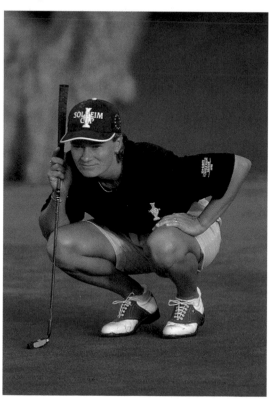

WIN THE HOLE
Although you are playing hole by hole against an opponent, play the course rather than her. Here, Catriona Mathew weighs up a putt during the Solheim Cup at Muirfield Village.

playing first, unless there is a set draw saying who should play. It is not correct simply for the lower-handicap player to go first.

➤ The player who wins the hole gets the 'honour' on the next tee and drives first. She keeps the honour until the other player wins a hole.

➤ Correctly, the player who is down should declare the score after each hole. This is not always done, but it should be. There is no need to keep a card of the match, provided this is done. In matchplay, you do not hole out and the hole by hole score is not relevant.

➤ If receiving a stroke when playing matchplay under handicap, the player receiving the stroke should announce this. She is responsible for claiming the stroke.

Rules for matchplay and strokeplay differ. In matchplay you are playing only against your opponent, whereas in strokeplay you are playing against the whole field.

It is not possible to go back and change the score. You must also state correctly the number of shots taken, if asked. If you do not, and do not correct the information before your opponent plays, you forfeit that hole. This is an example of a rule that does not apply in strokeplay. Try to grasp the difference in the rules.

The thinking side

This is very important in matchplay. As a general rule, try to play matchplay in the same way as you would strokeplay – in other words, just play the course and try to build up a good score without thinking too much about what your opponent is doing. If your opponent plays a bad shot, don't alter the way you play the next one. Don't change your approach to a hole until you know what your opponent has scored. It is very easy to assume she is going to hole a putt of, perhaps, 1.2m (4ft). If you are too bold with your 3-metre

(10-ft) putt and she then misses hers, you will probably miss yours as well.

It is very easy to be sidetracked by your opponent. Typically you see her drive out of bounds. Your first mistake is that you probably think 'Good!'. Your second mistake is that you change your driver to a 3 wood for safety. You then change your second shot from a 3 wood to a 7 wood, again for safety. Meanwhile your opponent crashes her ball onto the green in two more splendid shots, right by the hole. Put off by this, you take six, she takes five and you lose the hole. Easily done, and the match can be lost through that one silly error.

Remember that the match is not lost or won until the final putt is holed, and always think positively about the shot in hand, as you would in strokeplay. If you were five up and are suddenly only two up, forget what is past. Again, just live for the moment – the here and now. Remember, you cannot change what has gone before on the golf course.

Huge swings of fortune can take place in a match. You can be 5 up and lose; you can be 5 down and win. The golden rule is that, if you are the player who is up, you must never, ever feel sorry for your opponent – even if she is very young, very old or slightly tearful! She won't be feeling sorry for you. Don't relax or experiment with silly shots. Aim at winning by the biggest margin you can. Don't take any notice if she apologises for not giving you a game. The golf course and your own inadequacies give you a game and a challenge without any help from her.

Oh, and never ever wish your opponent ill. Don't hope she does a bad shot. If the next one is good you will be disappointed. Always assume the shot she is about to play will be perfect. That way you are lifted by her errors, and not demoralized by her successes. Concentrate on your own game.

REMEMBER PLAY THE COURSE, NOT YOUR OPPONENT

So You Want to Be a Winner?

Professionals often laugh about pupils who say 'I want to be a better golfer, but don't change my swing'. Perhaps, in reality, the pupil has a better understanding of the game than her professional! The first aim is to learn to do your best swing more often. The second is to learn the art of scoring and winning.

Winners on the pro circuit don't always have perfect swings. In fact they don't often have perfect swings. What they do have is self-belief and confidence, combined with a repetitive method.

To improve your golf, you need to understand your weaknesses. Monitor your results and see where the real problems lie.

On the course, plot your progress on the scorecard – not just in terms of your actual score, but in terms of achievements in other areas. If you improve certain elements of your game, the score itself will improve. On your scorecard, mark off the various columns and

use these to give yourself information.

Make one column the number of drives where you hit the fairway. Use the second column to mark how many greens you hit from under, say, 150 metres. In this way you begin to see whether your clubbing is accurate. Golfers will often find that they finish short of the flag on at least 15 or 16 of the holes. They never attack the hole.

In another column on the card you can assess your putting. How many putts did you take and from how far? Is the long putt short or past? See whether there is any pattern to your game that can be bettered without

BEING A WINNER
Sherri Steinhauer of the USA takes the trophy at the Women's British Open at Lytham St Anne's.

actually improving technique. It is only by keeping a record such as this and giving yourself feedback that you become aware of your own shortcomings.

Always try to practise by using a set schedule and give yourself a plan for your practice before you go out. Don't just hit balls aimlessly without having a set idea in mind. Think of a round of golf as, for example, 14 drives, four par threes, eight fairway woods, 10 medium or long irons, 10 short irons and so on. Keep a record of your practice and check the results. Note the grouping of the balls around your target. How many finish left and how many to the right? Are you achieving the distance you expect? How far do you hit the ball with each club, when you are using good golf balls?

Set yourself goals in order to improve. Determine what is the weakest part of your game and what is the strongest. List the five physical things that will most improve your game, in other words the type of shots, and then practise them. Learn to make friends with every one of your clubs. You should be on as good terms with your 4 iron as you are with your 5 iron (or any other club in the bag). That way your decision on clubbing isn't clouded by choosing the 5 instead of the 4 because you are on better terms with it.

If greater distance is your aim, be realistic. Everyone wants to hit the ball further – even Laura Davies. But don't try for another 30 metres and lose your rhythm. Try to hit the ball 10cm (4in) further, until those 10cm build into 10 metres. Be realistic. And if you want to hit the ball further, hit it louder!

Then clarify the five 'head' things to improve – confidence, judging distances, clubbing yourself, good preparation, choosing a target. Very often, real improvement comes not just from shotmaking but from factors far easier to correct. Break them down into small aims. If you want to break 80 for the first time,

don't look for the ultimate score. Set out to make 12 pars, for example. Try to make 3 birdies on every round. If just off the green at the first, think of it as a chip for your first birdie and not a struggle to save par. Think of holing long putts, chips, short pitches and you soon realize that the ones you miss will be closer than normal. Here are a few thoughts for learning to win – without changing your swing!

➤ I will learn the course and have no uncertainties as to distance.
➤ I will prepare my equipment well and have everything in my bag I need.
➤ I will choose the correct club on every shot and trust the yardage chart and club chosen.
➤ I will look like a winner to everyone watching me – whether winning or losing.
➤ I will keep my mind firmly in the present and play every shot to the best of my ability.
➤ I will make good, clear decisions, choosing a proper target for every shot.
➤ I will attack the golf course and pass the flag whenever I can and the situation allows.
➤ I won't search for excuses.
➤ I will find something good in every game of golf I play.
➤ I will learn to accept that golf is a game where bad shots are inevitable.
➤ I won't be angry with myself or show any anger or frustrations.

See the ability to score as an art all of its own. Enter every tournament you play with reality. If there are fifty other competitors it takes a lot to finish ahead of them. Don't pressurize yourself. See the game in context. Learning to win is a strange mixture of swing, shotmaking and scoring. The first, without the second and third, rarely, if ever, wins. The second and third with a repetitive, if imperfect technique, is often highly successful. Winning is often a question of making the bad shots better. True champions are those whose bad shots still receive praise from their playing partners.

REMEMBER
HIT IT, FORGET IT, WALK

Never assume that golfers don't need to be fit. For a professional or top-class amateur golfer, playing competitive golf requires mobility, strength and stamina.

A top golfer may put as much effort into a drive as a javelin thrower does in throwing a javelin. Over a 36-hole, one-day event, that may mean hitting over 20 drives at full strength, with some aggressively hit irons and fairway woods. The javelin thrower trains rigorously and meticulously for perhaps 12 throws in the day – and doesn't have to walk 10 miles at speed in between throws! Need I say more! If you want to be fit for a golfing season, walk, walk and walk some more. Use a treadmill at a gym through the winter – not running or even jogging – but walking at speed.

An average game of golf probably takes around four hours. Many players have nothing to eat or drink for an hour before that. It is a mistake. The body and brain need fuel to sustain performance. If you weren't on the golf course you would rarely go five hours or more without some form of fluid or nourishment. Don't assume that fluid intake is only required in the heat. Many golfers have a mental and physical crisis around the 12th

hole on the course. Tiredness sets in. Never expect to play good golf without taking on board both food and fluid during the round.

When you think of the golf swing, it requires flexibility. In the finish, your left foot stays pointing straight in front while your hips turn at right angles to this. Your ankles need looseness. Your back and waist need to be loose to turn and pivot. The left arm needs to work across the body towards your right shoulder, your wrists need to be flexible and your neck needs freedom to allow your head to stay still. Fortunately women have better mobility than men, but here are some exercises to help flexibility and strength.

Head and neck. Tip your head to the right as though touching your right shoulder with your right ear. Then tip it to the left, forwards and to the right. Shrug the shoulders up and down. Get rid of all the creaks and groans and feel the neck stretching.

Wrists. Just keep easing the thumbs back onto the inside of the wrists, and set them

STRETCHING
Conventional sports stretches – and even using a club and practice bag as props – will help maintain suppleness on the course.

back to form right angles (see the illustrations below). Encourage fliexibility by making fists and spreading your fingers as wide as possible.

Toe touching. Practise bending from the hips – the posture you need in the golf swing – touching your toes (see below, opposite). If you can do this with ease, try the same standing on the bottom step of a flight of stairs and ease the fingertips downwards.

Ham string stretch. Now move on to the legs. Put your right foot in front of you and squat down with your hands on your right knee. Put the left leg out straight behind you, with the left foot straight in front, forming a straight line along the left foot and right foot. Simply press down on the right knee and remain completely stationary for a few seconds. Don't bounce. Then repeat it with the other leg (see opposite).

Arms and fingers. To strengthen, try this very simple exercise. Simple hold the arms out at arm's length, with the fingers stretched. Pull the fingers in and out, in and out as fast as possible. It seems innocuous. But as you build up the numbers to 100 or more you will start feeling the good it is doing!

Another very simple exercise, which again has more effect than one would imagine, is to hold a golf club out at arm's length and to write your name in the air with the clubhead. Do it with each hand. It builds up strength and helps you make friends with the clubhead.

One of the most widely used exercises with women 'pros' is to attach a practice ball bag with a piece of rope to a club shaft or broom handle. Hold it out at arm's length and wind it upwards and downwards again (see below, opposite). Increase the number of balls in the bag as your strength develops.

If you are a fitness enthusiast, use a pair of dumb-bells and twist them in and out, first with the elbows supported and then without them supported. The first will exercise the upper arms, the second the lower arms.

Legs. To exercise your legs, stand with one foot on a firm chair. Push yourself slowly up and down on the leg. Then repeat it for the other leg. Another popular exercise for golfers is to hang your practice ball bag over your ankle and to lift the leg up and down (see below, opposite).

Remember that the simpler the exercises are, the more likely you are to repeat them. Done regularly, they will help you stay loose.

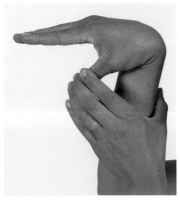

HANDS AND WRISTS

It is important to remain supple and loose in the hands and wrists for golf. Flexing your fingers and hands in the ways shown will help.

REMEMBER
DRINK PLENTY OF FLUID

Cards and Handicaps

Golf is a game with a unique system of scoring – 'handicapping' – which allows players of different abilities to compete on level terms with one another. Scores are recorded on golf cards.

In order to enjoy your golf and join in a club you need an understanding of pars, handicapping and scoring. First, let's take a player who is a good amateur of international standard. We will call her the scratch player. Par, or the standard scratch, is the measure of how she should play around a golf course.

On a hole of up to 200 metres (220 yards) or so for the ladies, we assume that the scratch player will hit the green in one shot and will take two putts. So we call this hole a par three. A par four, then, is anything from 201 metres (221 yards) to approximately 375 metres (410 yards), where we assume the scratch player will take two shots to get to the green, plus two putts, giving a par four. A par five is from approximately 376 metres (411 yards) and longer, where we assume our

Date	COMPETITION ABBOTSLEY OPEN				Tee		Handicap		Strokes Rec			
Player A	AUNDERS						SCR		—			
Player B	WORTHINGTON						15		15			
Markers Score	Hole	White Yds	Yellow Yds	Par	Index	Strokes Received A | B	Gross Score A | B	Result or Points	LADIES TEE Yards	Par	Index	
	1. Corncracker	337	331	4	13		4 5		321	4	15	
	2. Windy Ridge	367	360	4	9		4 4		353	4	7	
	3. Park Way	410	385	4	3		5 4		393	5	3	
	4. The Stumps	311	300	4	11		4 6		303	4	11	
	5. Saxons Hamlet	341	332	4	17		3 5		306	4	9	
	6. Mousehole	133	121	3	15		3 4		97	3	17	3 14
	7. Abbotsley Rise	298	284	4	7		4 5		269	4	13	4 8
	8. Downs	455	446	4	1		4 5		400	5	1	5 2
	9. Briar Hill	370	356	4	5		4 4		340	4	5	3 16
	OUT	3022	2915	35			35 42		2782	37		4 10
												5 4
	16. Barley Slice	450	382	4	2		4 5		397	5	6	
	17. Barford View	241	234	3	12		4 3		235	4	18	
	18. Final Fling	406	229	4	10		4 4		290	4	12	
	IN	3128	2865	35			36 37		2750	37		
	OUT	3022	2915	35			35 42		2782	37		
	TOTAL	6150	5780	70			71 79		5532	74		
	HANDICAP						— 15					
	NETT						71 64					

S.S.S WHITE 71 YELLOW 68 RED 72 PAR WHITE 70 YELLOW 70 RED 74

Markers Signature .... Players Signature ....

STROKEPLAY SCORECARD
A typical scorecard, filled in after a round of strokeplay.

scratch player will take three to reach the green, plus two putts again, making a par five. The lengths vary slightly from one country and one handicapping system to another. The par may also vary and not be judged solely on distance if, for example, the hole is played uphill or if there is some particular difficulty en route.

Adding the pars for each of the 18 holes gives the total par for the course. In most situations this is the same as the 'standard scratch' – the score for which our theoretical scratch player would complete the whole course. In the case of the card shown here, the standard scratch score (SSS) is 72. It is this total – the SSS – from which handicaps are assessed.

The scratch player, who hopes to go round in a score equal to the SSS, will be a player of amateur international or club professional standard.

A four handicap player would hope to go round in four shots more than the standard scratch, making her a player of roughly club or regional first team standard. The average woman golfer is, perhaps, 24 handicap and, in theory, anyone on that handicap should go round the course in 24 shots above the standard scratch. For the ladies, the maximum handicap is usually 45 – again varying from one country and system to another – meaning that a player would hope to go round in 45 shots above the standard scratch. But anyone with a higher score than this will still be given a 45 handicap. In most countries the maximum handicap for a man is 28.

Looking at the scorecard, you will see there are various columns. First is the column marked Yardage, which shows the distance of each hole, measured from a set point on the teeing ground to the centre of the green via the middle of the fairway. Some countries use metres or both yards and metres.

The next column shows the par of that hole based on its length and difficulty.

The column marked 'Stroke Index' is used in handicap competitions and is followed by the columns for completing the score. On the back of the card you will usually find the local rules and a column showing how to calculate handicaps for different competitions.

The column marked 'Stroke Index' is used when golfers play a match against each other, and also in some forms of competition, explained later, such as the Stableford Bogey or Bogey Competition. In a handicap match between, for example, a nine handicap and a 21 handicap, there is a handicap difference of 12. In a singles match you would take threequarters of this difference, giving a difference of nine.

Looking at this card, the 21 handicap player will receive a stroke from the lower handicap on each of those holes in the stroke index column which has the number nine or less against it. She receives nine shots in total from these holes, deducting one from each of her scores before matching it against her opponent's. If the match were halved and the players went down to the 19th, she would start taking strokes again on the same stroke index holes.

On the back of the card are details of the local rules. Common ones allow players to pick stones out of bunkers or to drop away from small, staked trees. The local rules give precise definitions of any out of bounds round the course.

The scorecard often has details of the handicap calculation used for foursome and singles matches and in the forms of Stablefords and Bogey competitions.

REMEMBER CHECK THE SCORECARD BEFORE SIGNING!

Competitions

There are competitions for four or more players in a group – useful on a day when the course is congested – and others that encourage speedy play or spare the diffident beginner the anguish of teeing off in front of the crowd at the first hole.

The standard games are described here, apart from strokeplay and matchplay, which have already been covered on pages 198–9 and 200–1. They can be the basis of more complex arrangements to suit the occasion.

Foursomes

In this, four golfers play together in pairs, but use one ball between a pair and take alternate shots for each hole. One player elects to drive the first hole and will then drive on every odd numbered hole; the other takes the even ones. This can then be played on a matchplay or strokeplay format. In America this is usually referred to as 'Scotch Foursomes'.

Four Ball Better Ball

This is a form of play in which four players play together, each using a ball. It is played in partnerships, matching the lower score of each of the partnerships in a matchplay format. Four ball better ball can also be played in strokeplay form. In a match, the handicapping is taken on a threequarter basis, the players taking handicap strokes from the lowest handicap of the four.

Greensomes

In this competition, players go out in fours, made up of two pairs. All four players drive on each hole. The players of each partnership choose the better drive of the two and finish the hole playing alternate shots, as in foursomes. The player whose drive was not taken plays the second shot. Some clubs use a handicap system for this, just taking the average of the two handicaps. Others use what is generally a fairer system, taking six-tenths of the lower handicap plus four-tenths of the higher handicap. A greensome can then be played as a match, a medal or a Stableford Bogey.

The Stableford or Stableford Bogey

This is a popular form of competition against par (derived from the old name for par of 'bogey'). In this, the player takes either full or seven-eighths of her handicap against par, according to the stroke index. (Some clubs use full handicap; others prefer seven-eighths.) In other words , assuming we use seven-eighths, a 24 handicap player would receive 21 strokes and gets one stroke on each hole plus a stroke on those in the index marked one, two or three.

On the card, she fills in the gross score and then, after mentally deducting the strokes, counts two points for a hole completed in par or nett par, one point for a score or nett score of one over par, three points for a birdie or nett birdie, four for an eagle or nett eagle, and so on. The player with the most points for the 18 holes wins, with the winning scores usually ranging from 35 to 42 points.

The Stableford form of competition can be played in singles, foursomes, four ball or greensomes.

Bogey Competition

This is an alternative to the Stableford Bogey and is, in effect, a matchplay competition in which the golfer plays a hole-by-hole match against par (bogey). The player receives threequarters of her handicap and takes those in the form of strokes from par according to the stroke index.

Unlike a true match, the whole round is completed and the player records on each hole whether, after receipt of her strokes, she has won or lost the hole against bogey. At the end of the round she records how many up or down she is against par, for example three up or six down. This is a difficult form of competition, with winning scores anything from two up to four down.

Bisque Bogey

In a match or bogey competition, an adaptation is to use 'bisques'. These are, in effect, strokes that can be taken where a player chooses, instead of at an allotted hole. In a Bisque Bogey the player would, for example, receive perhaps 15 strokes and could elect, after playing the hole, whether or not to take one of her bisques. In a similar way, a match can be played in which one player gives another six bisques and she can decide when she wants to take them.

Eclectic Competition

This is a type of competition run, as a rule, over a period of days, weeks or months, in which the player records her best score for every hole taken over that same period. There are various ways of playing an Eclectic Competition. In some cases, players are allowed unlimited cards and in others they are restricted. As a general principle, after completing the initial round, the player tries to improve the score for each individual hole before the usual deduction of half handicap.

Flag Competition

Here the player is allotted a certain number of strokes to use for the round, being the par of the course plus her handicap. In other words, a 20 handicap golfer playing on a par 70 course is given 90 strokes to use. She starts off from the first tee and, after playing 90 strokes, places a small flag with her name on

where the 90th shot finishes. The person who finishes nearest the 18th hole or farthest up the first or second fairway for the second time round is the winner.

St Andrews Greensome

The St Andrews Greensome is similar to an ordinary Greensome, except that the players alternate in taking the second shots. In other words, one player elects to take the second shot on the odd numbered holes and the other on the even ones. They still both drive and elect the better drive for the next player to play. Sometimes they are playing a second shot from their own drive, sometimes from their partner's.

Texas Scramble

This is a team competition, usually in teams of four. Each player drives off the first tee. The team captain then chooses the best drive and all the players take their ball to this position. They all then hit a shot from there. The captain again chooses the best second shot. Everyone else takes their ball to that spot and they continue until the first player has holed out. The use of handicaps in scrambles varies from one club to another with no rules set by golf's governing bodies.

Starting in competitions

Starting playing in competitions is a chicken and egg situation. You need a handicap to be allowed to compete and yet strokeplay is the most punishing form of competition. If you have the chance, join in with a club Texas Scramble. This is a friendly team competition in which you may be able to compete before you have a handicap. Once you have done the bare minimum to get your handicap, try to play in matches, Stablefords and Bogeys. They are far more fun, less demoralizing if you play badly, and a better way to start.

REMEMBER COMPETITIONS CAN BE FUN

Etiquette

Etiquette is very important on the golf course, so much so that it forms the first section of the Official Rules of Golf published by the Royal and Ancient Golf Club of St Andrews and the United States Golf Association. It is part of the tradition of golf, but is also important for safety.

Learn about golfing etiquette as soon as possible. Even if you are a novice golfer, you will then always be welcome on a golf course.

Here are some key points that are basically just good manners:
➤ Don't walk or move while others are playing.
➤ Always try to be aware of others playing behind you and let them through if you are holding them up. Remember that a player may hit the ball 225 metres (250 yards) and may be waiting for you, even though he/she seems a long way away. If you are losing ground on the match in front, be prepared to stand aside and wave other players on. Once you have waved them on, let them go. Particularly if you lose a ball, be quick in waving other players through.
➤ Always be punctual on the first tee. Don't damage the tee with practice swings.
➤ Replace divots and repair pitch marks on the greens.
➤ If you go into a bunker, always enter it from the back and never down the face unless your ball is right in the face. Rake the bunker well to smooth over your footprints. If there is no rake, use your clubhead.
➤ On the green, don't walk on the line of another player's shot. Always step carefully across it if you are going up to attend the flag. And when attending the flag, first see that it is loose and will pull out of the hole easily. Secondly, stand away from the hole to the side and don't cast your shadow over the hole. Thirdly, hold the flag to keep it from flapping in the wind. Finally, pull it out

immediately the player has struck her putt.
➤ State the score in a match at the end of every hole if you are the player who is down. If you are the one who is up, state the score if your opponent fails to do so.
➤ When marking your ball on the green, use a small coin or ball marker and place it behind the ball before picking it up. When replacing it, put the ball down in exactly the spot it came from and then pick up the marker. If, for some reason, you have to ask a player to mark her ball to the side, then remind her to replace it in the right spot.

Etiquette is also vital for safety
➤ Always stand to the right of the shot and never behind a player.
➤ On the tee, always go over to the right side of the tee to watch another player. This is crucial for safety. Remember that on a tee the other person may hit her drive, not be satisfied with it and then take a practice swing while you are possibly walking forward to take up your position. If you are on the correct, right side, you can start walking on to the tee earlier and in safety. If you stand on the wrong side you have to wait far longer to be safe.
➤ Never get ahead of a player, and never turn your back on someone who is playing, however expert. Always keep level with her and on the correct side.
➤ If there is any likelihood of your ball hitting someone else, or if it is going over trees towards an adjacent fairway, call out 'fore'.
➤ Always wait until the players in front are out of range. When hitting to the green, wait until they have cleared it and are well

ON THE GREEN
Always repair pitch marks on the green, do not walk over your opponent's line and respect their need for concentration. Pictured is Mayumi Hirase at Lytham St Anne's.

to the side before you play on.
➤ Finally, try to play golf at a reasonable speed. When you get to the tee, don't mark your card for the previous hole, if you are the first player to drive. Get on the tee as quickly as possible, but take time over your shot. Don't mark your card on the green or even by the green after finishing the hole.
➤ Get used to leaving your clubs on the correct side of the green as near as possible to the exit to the next tee.
➤ If you think you have lost a ball, get used to using the provisional ball rule. This will avoid the bother of having to go back to the tee. The rules state that you are allowed five minutes to look for your ball. Take no longer.

Courtesy shots
When playing in mixed golf, is there a correct formula for handicapping and courtesy shots? The whole idea of a handicap is that it allows players to compete on equal terms. Men and women play golf in a very different way. Most higher handicap men are hampered by lack of good direction; women are hampered by lack of distance. In matches or fourball games, men in a partnership will usually beat women. One man of the pair will probably play the hole well and the other badly. Both women will probably make the same score. For that reason alone courtesy

shots are often given based on past experience within the club of what creates a good, nail-biting match.

Generally courtesy shots should always be given by the men, firstly if they are playing off forward tees and not the tees from which their handicaps are calculated, and secondly if the standard scratch score for men is lower than for women. If the SSS for men is 70 and for women 73, some adjustment needs to be made. Generally the women would receive three courtesy shots, by nominally adding three to their handicap. There is no hard and fast rule and clubs vary in their interpretation of this. Hence its inclusion in etiquette rather than rules and handicapping!

REMEMBER
KEEP UP WITH
THE PLAYERS
IN FRONT

Points From the Rules

Golf has many different rules, some of them ancient, arcane and complex. Here are a few key points from the rules.

The ball should be played as it lies, which means that you cannot improve its lie, except on the tee. Here you can tread down behind it or pick pieces of grass from behind the ball, but you cannot do this anywhere else on the course.

Lost ball

If you lose a ball, play another one from the spot where the original one was hit and add a shot. This is known as 'stroke and distance'. In other words, if you lose a ball with your drive, the next one will be 'three off the tee'. If you lose a ball with your third shot, your next from the spot where you hit the lost ball from will be your fifth. Losing a ball is costly!

If you think you have lost a ball, you can play a 'provisional ball' up to the spot where you think the original one was lost. That could mean hitting more than one shot with it. State that you are playing a provisional ball. Don't just hit another or technically you are deemed to have counted the original as lost and it may not be. If the first ball is lost, you can go on with the provisional one. If the first ball is found, then the provisional one must be abandoned and you should go on with the first one or declare it unplayable.

Unplayable ball

If the ball is unplayable (through the green), which means anywhere other than hazards or the tee or the green of the hole being played, then you have three choices. The first is to take your ball out two club-lengths from its position no nearer the hole, drop it and add a penalty of one stroke.

Secondly, you can take stroke and distance and go back to the spot from where the original came. Thirdly, you can go back as far as you like, keeping the spot where the unplayable ball was between yourself and the flag.

In a bunker, you have the same options if the ball is unplayable. But if you are picking out two club-lengths or going back as far as you want, this must still be in the bunker. The only way you can pick out of a bunker is by taking stroke and distance, in other words going back to where the original shot came from. Remember that if you have one attempt at hitting out of the bunker and fail, you lose the stroke and distance option of being able to pick out of the bunker. Think first before losing this option.

The player is the sole judge of what is unplayable. What is unplayable to one person may be perfectly playable to another. No one can query your decision.

Identify your ball

Be careful to play the correct ball. Remember its make and number and, in competitions, put an identifying mark on it. Mark your ball with some identification – your initials or a characteristic blob! If you find another ball of the same make and number you will know whether it is yours. Remember a strange rule. If you find two balls of the same make and number and you don't know which is yours, the rules say you cannot say that either is yours and are deemed to have lost your ball!

If you play the wrong ball in strokeplay, you will be penalized two strokes for each shot you play with that wrong ball to a maximum of four strokes. If you play the wrong ball in matchplay, you lose a hole. If you play the wrong ball in a bunker, there is no penalty, providing you then identify it as being wrong and do not play any more shots with that ball outside the bunker. You can then go back and find the right ball.

Accidentally moving a ball

If you move a ball accidentally, penalties apply, other than on the green, where you replace the ball without penalty. Many golfers take a penalty in this situation when in fact they don't need to. Knowing the rules can save you shots.

The rules of golf are quite complex. For example, take the difference between an outside agency and a rub of the green. Assume that a dog picks up a stationary ball and runs off with it. You would replace it with no penalty. If a dog picks up a moving ball and runs off with it, unless you are on the green, this is known as a rub of the green and you simply play it from where the dog takes it. If it is lost altogether, then it must count as a lost ball. If, on the other hand, you have hit a ball with your putter on the green and a dog picks it up while it is moving, there is no penalty and you can replace and re-play it. Don't expect to know all the rules but be able to find them in the rule book.

WHAT TO DO WITH AN UNPLAYABLE BALL
If you deem your ball to be unplayable, you can take your ball out two club-lengths from its position no nearer the hole, drop it and add a penalty of one stroke. Rigo Higashio is shown during the Women's British Open at Woburn Abbey, England.

REMEMBER
ALWAYS KEEP A RULE BOOK IN YOUR BAG

More About the Rules

There are a number of other golf rules that you need to know about on a day-to-day basis.

Casual water

Basically, casual water and ground under repair should not be on the course. Casual water includes snow and ice and is all water lying on the course outside designated water hazards. You therefore have a free drop within a club-length of the nearest point of relief. You are permitted to play from the water or ground under repair if you prefer, unless there is a sign – GUR 'Play prohibited' – in which case you must take a drop. If you are on the green and water lies between you and the flag, you can move around to the side to take the nearest point of relief. But if you are chipping to the flag from off the green and there is water on the green in the way, you cannot get relief.

In the way

Obstructions can be either movable or immovable. What is movable to one person – a heavy bench for example – may be immovable to another. If movable – for example, the greenkeeper's rake or a drinks can – then you can move it, and there is no penalty if you should inadvertently move the ball. Movable obstructions are man-made items and do not include natural objects such as tree branches or twigs. If obstructions are immovable, then you must move the ball by finding the nearest point of relief, no nearer the hole, without measuring through the obstruction.

Over the water

There are two sorts of water hazard – standard and lateral. With a standard water hazard, you must cross it at some point. If your ball goes into it, you must take a penalty and can drop back as far as you like behind the hazard, keeping the point where the ball last crossed the hazard between you and the flag. But you must play your ball over the hazard. Remember about going back as far as you like. Don't drop too close on a down slope or area of rough. Take advantage of a little rules knowledge.

A lateral water hazard runs down the side of a hole. If you go in the water, you can pick the ball out again for a penalty shot and drop within two club-lengths on either side of the hazard, level with the point where the ball crossed the edge of the water. With water hazards you also have the option of stroke and distance and going back to the point from which you played the original shot. Many golfers forget that.

Ordinary water hazards should always be marked with yellow stakes or markers; lateral hazards are marked in red.

If your ball is lost in casual water, ground under repair or a water hazard, just treat it the same as if you had found the ball – drop outside the first two with no penalty, drop from the water hazard taking your penalty.

Teeing tips

Take care about playing from the wrong tee. Again, if you do so there is a penalty in both matchplay and strokeplay. If you play in the wrong order in a match – in other words taking the honour off the tee when your opponent should – or if you tee up from outside the tee, your opponent has the option of recalling your shot. If they recall your good shot, of course they risk your doing even better with the next one – perhaps even a hole in one! If your shot from the wrong place was a bad one, the chances are they won't even point out your error. They might, of course, point it out and mention that they won't bother to recall it! In strokeplay the latter would be a penalty.

Matchplay and strokeplay

It will pay dividends to learn all the differences between matchplay and strokeplay. In matchplay, once a hole has been completed and you have driven from the next tee, a retrospective penalty is generally not possible – except for finding extra clubs in your bag and serious misdemeanours that might result in disqualification. In strokeplay, if you do something wrongly on a hole and then drive off the next tee, it may not be possible to rectify the earlier error and this can result in disqualification. Playing the wrong ball and not discovering the error until halfway down the next fairway is an example. So take care.

Obstructions

A loose impediment is a natural object such as a leaf or twig, whereas a movable obstruction is something like a piece of paper, a cigarette end or a greenkeeper's rake. If a loose impediment is near your ball, other than on the green, take care before you move it. If you move anything within one club length of your ball and your ball moves, you incur a penalty – even if one doesn't seem to be the cause of the other. If you move something man-made and the ball moves, there is no penalty.

In a bunker you cannot move any natural object unless the local rule says to the contrary and allows you to remove stones. You can, however, remove movable obstructions – in other words, man-made items – without penalty, and would incur no penalty if your ball were moved in doing so.

Out of bounds

Golf courses cover large areas, but it is still possible to hit off the golf course altogether and be 'out of bounds'. Out of bounds is generally marked with white stakes. The scorecard may make other reference to out of bounds areas – such as obviously defined roads, walls, fences and so on. Even this requires clear interpretation. You can never move an out of bounds marker. They are immovable obstructions. The nearest, inside edge of the post marks out of bounds, but the whole of a ball has to be out of bounds for it to be out of bounds. Oh, and, yes, you can stand out of bounds to play a ball in bounds!

Governors of the game

Golf's rule book contains only 34 entries. But 'clubs' take up a page and a half of description and the specifications for the ball detail the tests that are applied (at 23ºC) to establish its legality, including maximum velocity off the tee.

The game has had formal rules since 1774. Since the 1890s, most of the world has acknowledged the Royal and Ancient Golf Club of St Andrews as the final authority. In recent years the Rules of Golf Committee, which invites representatives of the world's leading golfing nations to join it, has worked with the United States Golf Association, to provide a worldwide standardization of the rules.

A Decisions Sub-Committee answers queries. If they lead to interesting interpretations, loose-leaf revisions for the Rules of Golf are circulated around the world. A present concern, dealt with by another committee, is that new materials and technology used in the making of clubs and balls shall not give players unfair advantage or, indeed, defeat the object of established golf course design.

One rule change, in 1952, succeeded in removing the primary meaning of a colloquial word from the English language. A 'stymie' was the situation when an opponent's ball was on the putting surface between another player's ball and the hole. It could not be moved. Now it can, and the word stymie passed out of golf but endures in the language to describe other frustrations.

REMEMBER
KNOWING THE RULES SAVES SHOTS

Glossary

A

Address The golfer's position when preparing to hit the ball.

Airshot Swinging at the ball and missing completely.

Albatross A hole completed in three shots less than par; also known as a 'double eagle'.

All square In MATCHPLAY, when players are even in the match.

Approach shot One whose target is the green.

Approach putt Not aimed directly at the hole but 'laying up' close enough to make the next putt a certainty.

B

Backspin The spin on the ball applied by the loft on the clubface. A skilled player may apply extra backspin to stop the ball rolling forward on landing.

Backswing The first half of the swing, when the club is taken away from the ball in preparation for the THROUGHSWING.

Better ball When the lower score in a partnership is recorded for each hole.

Birdie A hole that is completed in one under par.

Bisque In a match played to handicap, a stroke which can be claimed where the competitor chooses, rather than at allotted SCORE INDEX holes. It is taken after the hole is played.

Blaster Alternative, old fashioned name for the most lofted club, the sand wedge.

Bogey A hole completed in one over par; formerly, in Britain, an alternative name for par.

Bogey competition The player receives three quarters of handicap and records performance against par, e.g. 2 up (on par), 3 down (on par).

Borrow The slope of the green's surface; in response, the player 'borrows' to the left or right.

Bunker A depression in the ground, usually, but not always, filled with sand, designed to catch mis-hit balls. In the US, also known as a 'trap' or 'sand trap'.

Bye Unofficial match played over the rest of the course when a MATCHPLAY competition has been won before the 18th hole has been played.

C

Caddie A helper who carries a player's bag around the course and may advise on the course or the game.

Carry The distance a struck ball travels through the air. Also the distance over any rough or other obstacle to the fairway or chosen landing spot.

Casual water Water on the course, including snow and ice, which is not part of the design, such as rain puddles or over-irrigated areas. If a ball is in such water or, to play it, the player's feet would be, one can take a free DROP. If there is casual water on the green, a ball on the green may be moved to the nearest place equally distant from the hole from which a putt will avoid water.

Centre-shaft Style of putter in which the shaft attaches to the middle of the head.

Chip A short running shot with a medium iron from just off the edge of the green.

Closed A relationship between the direction of the stance and the clubface. The clubface is 'closed' or 'shut' if it is angled toward the feet; the stance is 'closed' if the front foot is across the target line.

Cup The tubular lining sunk in the hole. Also, the hole itself.

D

Dead A ball so close to the hole that it can be assumed the next putt is unmissable; in MATCHPLAY that putt is conceded.

Divot The sliver of turf cut after the ball is struck by a well-hit iron shot.

Dormie In MATCHPLAY, when a competitor leads by as many holes as there are left to play, e.g. 4 up with 4 to play.

Downswing The part of the golf swing from the top of the backswing to striking the ball.

Draw A shot with a slight, controlled curve through the air, from right to left (right-handed player).

Driver The 1 wood, the most powerful club in the set, used for getting maximum length off the tee.

Drop When a ball must be lifted, under penalty or otherwise, the player, standing erect, holds the ball at arm's length and shoulder height and drops it not nearer the hole.

E

Eagle A hole completed in two under par.

Eclectic A competition over several rounds, weeks or months, in which players record their best scores on every hole of the course.

Explosion shot The shot at a ball which is embedded in the sand of a bunker.

F

Face The surface of the clubhead that strikes the ball. Also the sheer bank in the front of a bunker.

Face insert The extra hard impact area set into the face of a wooden club – where wood is still used.

Fade A shot designed to curve slightly in the air, from left to right (right-handed player).

Fairway The cut grass, and proper route, between tee and green.

Fairway woods 2, 3, 4, 5, 7 and 9 and sometimes higher-numbered woods designed to be used when the ball is in play after the tee shot.

Flag The marker that shows the position of the hole on the green.

Flag competition Each competitor plays the number of shots derived from adding par for the course to their handicap. The player who gets the farthest (marking the place with a flag) is the winner.

Flange The broad sole of an iron club, particularly exaggerated on a sand wedge.

Flat swing One in which the club's plane around the body is low.

Followthrough The part of the swing beyond impact with the ball.

'Fore' The shouted word by which golfers warn others on the course that they are in danger of being hit by a ball.

Fourball Match between four players,

usually two a side, using a ball each. The better score of each team at each hole counts.

Foursome Match between two pairs of players, each side playing one ball and taking alternate shots. Tee shots are taken alternately.

Fringe The collar of slightly longer grass around the close-mown putting surface of the green.

G

Grain The angle at which the grass of a green grows. Putting 'against the grain' requires much more effort than 'with the grain'.

Green The closely mown, carefully manicured target area in which the hole is cut.

Greensomes Type of match for pairs of players. Both players drive at each hole, choose the better drive and then continue the course with alternate shots. The handicap used by each side is six-tenths of the lower handicap and four-tenths of the higher.

Grip The position of the hands on the club. It also describes the leather binding or rubber sleeve by which the clubshaft is held.

Gross score The number of shots taken to complete the course, before deduction of handicap to give the nett score.

Ground under repair Area of a course temporarily out of play, from which a ball may be removed for a DROP without penalty; a ball outside the area may also be moved if the lie would cause the player to stand in it.

H

Half When opponents register the same score. A match is 'halved' if it is completed all square.

Handicap Rating of a player's skill relative to par for the course. A 20-handicap player should complete a par 70 course in a score of 90. This stroke allowance permits players of unequal skill to compete on equal terms.

Hanging lie When the ball is on ground sloping down ahead of the player.

Hazard Lakes, ponds and ditches (water hazards) or sand bunkers. You cannot ground the club before playing a shot from a hazard.

Heel The part of the clubhead beneath the end of the shaft.

Hole The hole, 4 ¼ inches in diameter, into which the ball is played.

Honour To play first off the tee, the privilege of the winner of the preceding hole.

Hooded When the clubface is turned CLOSED and inward, reducing its loft.

Hook Faulty stroke when the ball curves to the left (right-handed player).

Hosel The extension to the clubhead into which the shaft fits.

IJKL

Lateral water hazard A ditch stream or pond roughly parallel to the line of the hole, marked with red stakes. A ball picked out may be played from either side, with a one stroke penalty.

Lie The position in which the ball comes to rest; also, the angle between the clubhead and shaft which may vary to suit short and tall players.

Links A seaside golf course, typified by sand, turf and coarse grass, of the kind where golf was originally played along the east coast of Scotland.

Local rules Clarification of points about unusual features or obstacles on a course, itemized on the back of the scorecard.

Loft The angle on the clubhead which enables the player to produce more or less height; also, to make the ball rise.

Long game The shots in which achieving distance is important.

Loose impediments Twigs and leaves, not actually growing, and not adhering to the ball, which may be removed from around it without penalty. The ball itself must not be moved in the process.

Lost ball If after five minutes searching a ball cannot be found, a competitor is penalized one stroke and plays another ball from the spot where the first one was hit, counting as the third shot.

MN

Mark To identify the spot on the green where a player has picked up a ball for cleaning or to clear the way for another player's putt.

Marker The player who keeps a record of another's score.

Matchplay Contest decided by the number of holes won rather than the total number of shots.

Medal play Strokeplay; contest decided by the lowest number of shots.

Nett score A player's score for a round after the handicap allowance has been deducted.

O

Open Of the clubhead, when it is turned out at the toe; of the stance, when the line of the feet is to the left of the target (right-handed player).

Out of bounds Ground officially outside the playing area, marked by lines of posts or fences. A ball hit into it must be replayed from the original spot, and a penalty stroke is added.

PQ

Par The number of shots a scratch player is expected to take on a hole or a course.

Penalty In strokeplay, a rule infringement usually costs two strokes; in matchplay, the hole is generally lost.

Pin Informal name for the flagstick in the hole.

Pitch shot A short shot to the green, hit high so that it will not roll on landing.

Provisional A ball played when it seems likely that the preceding shot is lost or out of bounds. It will count, plus a penalty stroke and the first stroke, if the original ball is not found; if it is, the provisional cannot be used.

Pull A straight shot to the left of the target (right-handed player).

Push A straight shot to the right of the target (right-handed player).

Putt The rolling shot taken on the green, with a putter.

R

Rough The area of less kempt grass and

other low-growing vegetation bordering the fairway.

Rub of the green When a ball is stopped or deflected accidentally. It has to be played where it lies, except on the green.

Rules The world of golf is administered by the Royal and Ancient Golf Club of St Andrews (the R and A) and the United States Golf Association (USGA). Local rules may be set by a club to cope with peculiarities on its course.

S

Sand trap In the US, a bunker.

Sand wedge The most lofted iron club in the set, for playing bunker shots and pitches.

Scratch player One who is expected to play the course in par.

Set of clubs The maximum allowed is 14, usually 4 woods, 9 irons 1 putter.

Shank Area of an iron's clubhead at the HOSEL; hence a shot hit by the clubface at this point, which flies off to the right (right-handed player).

Short game Approach shots to the green, and putting.

Shut See CLOSED.

Singles One player against another.

Slice Faulty shot which curves left to right in the air (right-handed player).

Socket See SHANK.

Sole The underside of the clubhead.

Square The position of the body at the ADDRESS when it is parallel to the line of the ball to the target.

Stableford A form of competition against par, using full or ⅞ths of handicap according to the stroke index. Nett par scores 2 points; one over, 1 point; a birdie, 3 points.

Stance The player's position when the feet are set, in alignment, ready to play the ball.

Standard Scratch Score The assessment of par for a course and the basis for handicapping.

Stroke A shot in golf.

Stroke and distance The penalty of one stroke and the return to the site of the shot before, when a ball is lost, out of bounds or otherwise unplayable.

Stroke index The numbers on a scorecard indicating the order of the holes at which a handicap player receives strokes.

Strokeplay Competition decided by the number of shots taken.

Swingweight Measure of balance and overall weight of clubs; in a matched set, all clubs should feel the same when swung.

T

Tee, teeing ground Flat, sometimes raised, area from which first shots at each hole are played. There may be several: men's competition tee ('the tiger tee'), men's tee, forward men's tee and ladies' tee.

Texas scramble Team competition in which all players play from the site of their team's best drive, best second shot, and so on.

Three off the tee If a ball is lost, out of bounds or unplayable from the tee shot, the player is penalized one stroke and tees off again – the third shot.

Throughswing The part of the swing during which the ball is actually hit.

Through the green The golf course, apart from teeing grounds and putting green of the hole being played and all hazards on the course.

Toe The area of the clubhead farthest from the shaft.

Top To hit the ball above its centre; a topped shot does not rise off the ground.

Trap In the US, a bunker.

U

Unplayable A player may choose to deem a ball unplayable, taking a penalty stroke and DROPPING the ball no nearer the hole. A ball that is unplayable in a bunker must be dropped in the bunker or STROKE AND DISTANCE taken.

Uphill lie When the ball is positioned on ground sloping up ahead of the player.

Upright Swing style in which the clubhead movement is almost vertical.

VW

Waggle A player's loosening-up movements at address.

Wedge A club with an extremely lofted face: pitching and sand irons.

Whipping The closely bound binding at the head of a wooden club.

Wrist cock The natural hinging of the wrist which begins as the club is lifted on the backswing.

Credits and Acknowledgments

Produced by Focus Publishing, The Courtyard, 26 London Road, Sevenoaks, Kent TN13 1AP

Artwork by Pamela Goodchild

Computer graphics by Focus Publishing

Studio photography by Laura Wickenden

The author and publishers would like to thank Wendy Dicks and Sarah Greenall, who modelled for many of the photographs.

Stock photography credits:
ActionPlus: pp. 22/3 (Chris Brown); p.213 (Glyn Kirk)
Allsport: pp.118/9, 211 (David Cannon); pp.147, 195 (Harry How); p.143 (Andy Lyons); pp.55, 81, 94/5 (Stephen Munday); pp.50, 56/7, 186/7 (Andrew Redington)
Peter Dazeley: pp. 63, 84, 113, 129, 173, 180, 196
Eric Hepworth: p.7
Mark Newcombe: pp. 9, 10
Phil Sheldon: pp. 154, 174, 194, 199, 200
Phil Sheldon/Jan Traylen: pp. 132/3, 149, 165, 168/9, 202
The Stock Market/Ed Bock: p.111